The Management Challenge

The Management Challenge

Japanese Views

Edited by Lester C. Thurow

The MIT Press
Cambridge, Massachusetts
London, England

Second printing, 1986

© 1985 by The Massachusetts Institute of Technology

This book was set in VIP Baskerville by Village Typographers, Inc., and printed and bound by The Murray Printing Company in the United States of America.

Library of Congress Cataloging in Publication Data

Main entry under title:

The Management challenge.

Includes index.
1. Management—Japan—Addresses, essays, lectures.
I. Thurow, Lester C.
HD70.J3M264 1985 658′.00952 84-28881
ISBN 0-262-20053-8

Contents

Contributors

Saburo Okita

Dr. Okita is chairman of the Institute for Domestic and International Policy Studies, which he founded in March 1981. He is also adviser to the Minister of Foreign Affairs, the Economic Planning Agency, the Science Technology Agency and the Environment Agency. Dr. Okita is special adviser to the International Development Center of Japan and to the Japan Economic Research Center (JERC) of which he was president and chairman. He was president of the Overseas Economic Cooperation Fund (OECF, 1973–77), foreign minister (November 1979–July 1980) and government representative for External Economic Relations (July 1980–December 1981). Dr. Okita was director general of the Overall Planning Bureau of the Economic Planning Agency in the 1950s and 1960s when Japan formulated and implemented its Doubling of National Income Plan (1960). He is president of International University of Japan and is the author of many articles and books in English and Japanese, on Japan's economy and international economic problems.

Toshimasa Tsuruta

Professor Tsuruta is a professor of economics at Senshu University, Japan. He is also senior economist of the Research Department at the Research Institute of National Economy. He was a member of the Antitrust Act Research Council in Japan's FTC (a private advisory committee for the chairman of the FTC, 1978–82) and is a member of Economic Research Council for the Antitrust Policy in Japan's FTC (1982–), a chairman of the Distribution Policy for the Antitrust Act Research Council in the FTC (1983–). Professor Tsuruta has authored *Postwar Japan's Industrial Policy* and coauthored a number of books on the industrial structure and economic policies of Japan.

Hisao Kanamori

Since 1973 Mr. Kanamori has served as president of the Japan Economic Research Center, previously as its chief economist from 1967–70. Past professional experience also includes positions as deputy director and chief of the Domestic Economic Research Division of the Economic Planning Agency of Japan. Mr. Kanamori earned his degrees from Tokyo University and Nuffield College, Oxford University, subsequently has taught at Tokyo University, Waseda University, Gakushuin University, and Tokyo University on various aspects of the Japanese economy.

Munemichi Inoue

Mr. Inoue is a lecturer of economics at Saitama University, Japan, and manager of the Economic Research and Information Department at the Marubeni Corporation. He studied sociology and economics at Hitotsubashi University, the Japan Economic Research Center, Tokyo, and Cambridge University. His professional experience includes being fellow and visiting scholar of the Center for International Affairs at Harvard University 1979–81.

Hiroyuki Itami

Professor Itami is presently an associate professor at the Department of Commerce, Hitotsubashi University. From 1975–76 and 1982–83, he was a visiting assistant and associate professor at the Graduate School of Business, Stanford University. He has received a bachelor's degree and a Master of Commerce degree from Hitotsubashi University, Tokyo, and a Ph.D. of Industrial Administration at Carnegie-Mellon University. Professor Itami's teaching and research interests include corporate strategy and economic analysis of internal organization and comparative management. He has received numerous honors and awards for his publications, including "The Best Literature in Economics and Management Award for 1981" and "The Management Science Literature Award" for 1981.

Haruo Shimada

Professor Shimada is professor of economics at Keio University, Japan. He received bachelor's and master's degrees from Keio University and a Ph.D. from the University of Wisconsin-Madison. He also served as visiting principal research officer of Economic Planning Agency and is serving as a member of special committees of both Economic Advisory Council and Employment Advisory Council. He has written widely on Japanese labor-management relations and their implications for economic growth.

Hiroshi Takeuchi

Mr. Takeuchi is managing director and chief economist of the Long-Term Credit Bank of Japan, Ltd. He was a lecturer of economics at Tokyo University where he earned his degree from the Economics Department. Mr. Takeuchi is the author of many books on Japanese economics and industry. He is the chairman of the Specialists Commission of Circulation (Keidanren) and advisor to Labor Questions Research Committee (Nikkeiren).

Masakazu Yamazaki

Professor Yamazaki is professor at Osaka University, Japan, where he specializes in Theater Studies. His past teaching experience includes professor of literature at Kansai University, Japan, and visiting professor at Columbia University. He received a bachelor's degree and a Master of Literature degree from Kyoto University, Japan, and has studied at Yale Drama School. Professor Yamazaki has written a number of books and papers on the character of the Japanese and comparisons between Japan, Western Europe, and the United States.

Takashi Kiuchi

Mr. Kiuchi is the general manager of planning and administration of the International Operations Group at Mitsubishi Electric Corporation. His past experience at Mitsubishi includes positions as manager of Overseas Market Planning; executive vice president of Mitsubishi Electric Sales America; western regional manager, MGA Division; Osaka Sales Office. Mr. Kiuchi received his bachelor's degree from Keio University and master's degree from the University of British Columbia. In 1980 he participated in the Program for Senior Executives at the MIT Sloan School of Management.

Ichiro Hattori

Since 1979 Mr. Hattori has been president of Daini Seikosha Co., Ltd., which became Seiko Instruments & Electronics Ltd. in 1983; president of Suwa Seikosha Co., Ltd., since 1980; and, since 1972, a director of the board of K. Hattori & Co., Ltd., which became Hattori Seiko Co., Ltd. in 1983. Mr. Hattori is chairman of Epson Corporation and a director of the board of various overseas subsidiaries of Seiko and Epson. Mr. Hattori studied economics at the University of Zurich and at Yale University·where he received a Master of Economics degree. He also received a Bachelor of Law degree at Tokyo University. Mr. Hattori has many philanthropic affiliations in Japan and abroad and has written numerous publications on Japanese management, economics, and corporate structure.

Shoichi Royama

Professor Royama is a professor of monetary theory at Osaka University, Japan. He has received a bachelor's and a master's degree from Tokyo University and a Ph.D. of Economics from Osaka University. He was a visiting research fellow at the University of Washington 1979–80. He has authored and coauthored books and papers on Japan's financial mechanism and banking behavior. For his recent book, *The Financial System in Japan,* he has received the "Economist Award for 1983."

The Management Challenge

Introduction

After World War II and until the late 1970s the United States had a huge economic and technological lead over the rest of the world. Leaving Canada aside, America's per capita GNP was twice that of any other industrial country in the world. American firms were world technological leaders in almost everything. When it came to basic research, there were no competitors. America enjoyed effortless superiority.

It was not always so. In the eighteenth and nineteenth centuries the United States was far behind Great Britain economically. America started off as a copier. New England's textile mills hired craftsmen (we would now call them engineers) who had worked in, or toured, the British textile mills and had memorized or written down enough of what they had seen to copy those mills in the New World. American history schoolbooks remember this copying as a good example of Yankee ingenuity. British history schoolbooks see it in another light: as theft. Americans stole British technology.

Throughout the nineteenth century American firms were famous for borrowing technologies. The great French observer of the American scene, Alexis de Tocqueville, describes America as a land of copiers, but copiers who quickly made products better than the original. Ideas, such as the Bessemer steel process, were developed abroad but brought to America and then changed to turn out slightly cheaper or better products than those produced in Europe. Starting from far behind, the American per capita GNP finally caught up with that of Great Britain around 1900. From then on, America had to invent rather than copy.

America was not a world leader in basic knowledge until after World War II. Until that time most basic scientific breakthroughs were made in Europe. Without World War II it is also doubtful that America would have caught up as fast as it did. The war destroyed Europe's basic scientific facilities in both physical and human terms. Some of Europe's most productive minds—Einstein, Fermi—were literally exported to the United States.

America's effortless superiority is over. Other countries have caught up with us economically—one can argue as to whether their per capita GNPs are slightly ahead or slightly behind us—and American firms are no longer the world's technological leaders in everything. Leadership has moved abroad in such industries as shipbuilding, steel making, consumer electronics, and automobiles. America still leads in basic science, but even there its position is being challenged.

To a great extent our large postwar lead was an artificial product caused by the destruction of the war. Americans are not that much smarter than everyone else, so their enormous economic and technological leadership inevitably was going to disappear as the rest of the world recovered from the war. In many ways the loss of this leadership is positive; it is preferable to live in a neighborhood with other wealthy people than in a neighborhood with poor people even if you are occasionally envious of your neighbors. But at the same time Americans do not want to fall substantially behind and gradually become a relatively poor country, which has happened to some former world economic leaders such as Great Britain. We want to be able to run even with the leaders of the economic pack.

To catch up, the rest of the world obviously had to have a period of time when its productivity grew faster than that in America. But there comes a time, and it is now, when Americans have to reaccelerate their rate of productivity growth to equal that of the world leaders. And since Japan is the leader when it comes to industrial productivity, this means reaching parity with Japanese productivity growth.

To meet this objective will require some fundamental rebuilding of American institutions and practice. No one can build a high-quality economy out of low-quality components. To compete, our workers, managers, investments, and governments will have to be equal to those of the best in the world. A case can be made that in each of these areas we have fallen behind. America has more illiterates and fewer engineers per capita than Japan. American personal savings rates are a third of those in Japan. American government often seems to impede economic progress rather than help it. A failure in any component leads to a failure in the final product. Although significant upgrading will be needed in each of these components, this book focuses primarily on one component: the management component.

In the auto industry it has long been standard operating procedure to buy a competitor's cars, disassemble them, and see what can be learned that would make your next car better. The aim is not to copy a competitor's car but to pick up bits and pieces—ideas—that can be used, or more likely modified, to make your next car better. This was once the American way; it is the Japanese way, and it will have to become the American way again. We lost the habit during the long period of time when there was legitimately little to be learned from the way that our competitors' economies or products were constructed.

In disassembling the metaphysical car, there are two approaches. An outsider can rip the car apart and report on how he thinks it was put together. In dissecting America the great outsider was de Tocqueville. Bringing outside

French eyes to the problem, he could see things about how nineteenth-century America was put together that Americans could not themselves see. The second approach, possible only with luck, is to persuade a generous insider to help you disassemble the car and explain how it was put together. Both approaches have merit, but we are lucky enough to be able to follow the second one in this book. Twelve Japanese have agreed to share their insights as to how Japanese firms are managed—to disassemble the car.

The American and Japanese economic stories start from a very different historical point. In Japan, a strong central government existed long before the industrial revolution began in the 1880s, and after World War II only one institution existed: government. In this case only an American government existed, but nonetheless it was a government. Given such a history, it is not surprising that government did, and does, play an important role in planning the economy. Firms grew in a context where government was important to economic success. Government was the guiding figure without whose cooperation economic success was impossible.

By contrast, American history began on an empty frontier without government. The industrial revolution began in the United States at a time when, for all practical purposes, there was no government when it came to economics. Customs duties on foreign products were the only significant government economic function. At the beginning firms were much stronger than government. Government was not even a younger partner in stimulating economic growth, but an adversary. It was an adversary because American government grew up in response to the challenges and problems created by powerful firms.

In the late nineteenth century the growth of the great trusts (railroads, steel, oil) led to the growth of government as an economic regulator; the Interstate Commerce Commission was established and the antitrust laws enacted. Thus government grew up as a device for controlling the abuses of large firms, not as a partner. The next expansion of government followed in the wake of the industrial failures of the Great Depression. Since the free market economy did not work, government inherited a role as a macroeconomic planner. Finally those left behind by the private economy (the unemployed, the unskilled, the poor) led to the growth of the welfare state—the New Deal in the 1930s and the Great Society in the 1960s. Government stepped in where the market failed, but each of those steps was resented by the proponents of unfettered free markets.

Given this adversarial history, it is not surprising that Americans have much to learn in the area of cooperative business-government relations to promote economic growth. And there is no one better able to disassemble this part of the car than Saburo Okita, former foreign minister and head of the Japanese Economic Planning Agency during the income-doubling decade of the 1960s.

Successful economies begin, however, not with government but with people. All institutions—governments and firms—are in the end no better, or worse, than the people who design and operate them. Just as a successful economy begins with a high-quality, well-motivated, cooperative labor force, so this book begins with an analysis of the problems of people management. It is in people management—soft productivity as opposed to the hard productivity of more investment or research and development—that American management seems to be failing. The Japanese seem to be able to get more productivity out of their workers in Japan, and perhaps in America. Our folklore now abounds in dramatic tales of Japanese successes with American workers, such as at the Sony plant in San Diego or the Matsushita (Quasar) plant in Chicago.

The reasons for Japanese success with people management are controversial even among the Japanese. Some see it as a matter of culture, others as a matter of incentives. Both views are set forth in this book. From the cultural point of view the Japanese have a long history of emphasizing the group rather than the individual. The search for social consensus is a Japanese art form even more highly developed than the tea ceremony. Hiroshi Takeuchi, in his chapter on motivation and productivity, sees traditional Japanese culture as the source of good people management. To bring out the cultural factors even more clearly, Masakazu Yamazaki, an expert on comparative culture, analyzes the cultural characteristics that set the environment within which Japanese managers manage.

But seniority promotions, lifetime employment, and a wage structure heavily conditioned by bonuses also provide an incentive system where it is individually rational for one to obtain skills and to cooperate as a well-motivated employee. One maximizes one's own current bonus and lifetime income by doing so. Haruo Shimada emphasizes the importance of these incentives on good people management.

While both incentives and culture are undoubtedly important in generating a well-motivated, cooperative labor force, there are in all probability a variety of cultures and incentives that can lead to the same desirable end result of a productive labor force. The problem is to blend the right ingredients in the right proportions. And it is from this perspective that we should look at the Japanese blend. What does it tell us about reblending our own mixture of culture and incentives?

If one looks at current American ingredients and proportions in contrast with those of Japan, some differences immediately stand out. The Japanese, with their emphasis on lifetime employment, have very little turnover. At one point during the Sloan School-Suntory Foundation conference at MIT, Takashi Kiuchi, the general manager of international operations at Mitsubishi Electric, was asked if any of his employees stationed abroad had ever left to work for another employer. He was unable to think of any losses. In contrast, the average turnover rate in American manufacturing is 4 percent per month. Almost 50 percent of the labor force of the typical American firm quits or is fired every twelve months. To a Japanese manager, the American turnover rate is probably the most disturbing fact about the American economy. The initial response is to ask how anyone can manage given such turnover rates.

How do you get cooperation and a willingness to sacrifice for the long-run good of the company when almost no one—managers or workers—is going to be around in the long run to enjoy the fruits of that sacrifice and cooperation? What company is going to pay to have its employees learn foreign languages if employees quit right after they have acquired a new skill at company expense? Yet how can a company compete in foreign markets if its employees do not know foreign languages? What employees are going to invest in a new skill that will benefit their company, such as learning an obscure language, if they are in danger of being laid off? Yet how can a company compete if its employees do not invest in the new skills that the company needs? Several hundred Japanese study at MIT at company expense. How many Americans study at the University of Tokyo at company expense? Few, if any.

Under American conditions it is not necessary, or perhaps even desirable, to achieve zero turnover, but it is reasonable to ask whether we have not overemphasized personal mobility. If so, clearly it is posible to restructure our incentive system to reduce turnover.

Whatever the culture, cooperation is a matter of establishing a structure of mutual allegiances. Consider lifetime employment. Only about 40 percent of the Japanese work force have it. Most American firms have seniority layoffs; this means that at least 40 percent of the American work force has de facto lifetime employment. For all practical purposes these American workers will not be fired unless the firm goes broke, but this is all that any Japanese is guaranteed. The difference is that an explicit guarantee of lifetime employment provides a sense of economic security and mutual obligation that our seniority system does not seem to provide.

Consider the differences in reaction when the Mazda (Toyo Kogo) Corporation was threatened with bankruptcy in the early 1970s and when Braniff Airlines did not go broke in the early 1980s. In Mazda's case, workers and managers agreed to take a 50 percent cut in pay to save the company, but everyone was kept on the payroll. The Braniff workers and managers would not agree to a 10 percent cut in pay despite the fact that they were told that the company would go out of business, as it did, if they refused. Workers believed that they would be laid off with, or without, a 10 percent wage cut, and if they were going to be unemployed anyway, they might just as well be fired from a high-paying job as from a low-paying job. Yet is there any doubt as to which of these reactions has the best long-term survival characteristic?

Most public opinion polls find that more economic security is the primary demand of the American work force in both good and bad times. Yet our system of employment seems to deny employees precisely what they most want. Those who believe that they, or their friends, will be laid off whenever they are not needed are going to reciprocate and be willing to quit whenever a better opportunity appears or whenever the employer needs sacrifices by workers.

Cooperative labor-management relations are forged in good times, not in bad times. This is hardly a startling insight but one that the Japanese seem to have remembered and we have forgotten. The current American pattern of "give-backs" extracted from a reluctant labor force under economic duress should not be seen even as the beginning of cooperation. Cooperation is a two-way process, and any willingness to maintain employees on the payroll in exchange for give-backs has been notable by its absence.

Nowhere is the absence of mutual respect and cooperation more clearly seen than in the American pattern of layoffs. Professor Robert McKersie has noted that 90 percent of the American companies who had laid off blue-collar workers for economic reasons in the recession of the early 1980s had not laid off a single white-collar worker. That description is one of a class society with an unfair sharing of economic burdens. And whatever the country or culture, class societies with an unfair distribution of economic burdens are never cooperative societies.

Nowhere is the difference in people management more pronounced than in the manner in which firms treat their human losers, those workers who fail to perform for whatever reason—motivation, alcohol, mental illness. In Japan the firm is expected to play a primary role in taking care of and helping to rehabilitate them. In America the losers are fired and become a government responsibility. Is it any surprise that Japanese firms get more loyalty from the losers and, more important, from their fellow workers?

Patterns of labor-management relations also have implications that extend far beyond that of direct labor-management issues. As Hiroyuki Itami points out, they lead to a very different pattern of investment decisions. The American firm is driven by a capital-pull imperative in deciding on what new areas to enter. It goes where the rate of return on investment is highest, given constraints imposed by its ability to hire workers with the necessary qualifications. By contrast, the Japanese firm is driven by a labor-push imperative. It looks at its labor force and then moves into new areas that will utilize the skills of its labor force, given constraints imposed by a need to obtain investment funds. Both sides are maximizers subject to constraints, but the maximand and the constraints are exactly reversed.

Americans take pride in their efficient capital markets and force the labor market to adjust to whatever capital flows it produces. The result is an efficient capital market but an inefficient labor market. What is considered full employment in the United States is far above what is considered full employment in any other industrial country, and since World War II American unemployment has been far above that in Japan.

The Japanese take pride in their efficient labor market and force the capital market to adjust to the realities of labor supplies as best it can. Americans thus describe the Japanese capital markets as horribly inefficient. From an American perspective Japanese firms accept low rates of return and funds are inefficiently allocated across the economy rather than efficiently flowing to the areas with the highest rates of return.

Which set of objectives and constraints has the greatest payoff in the long run? Based on the evidence accumulated during the past thirty years, the question must be decided in the Japanese favor: their economy has outperformed ours. But here as everywhere else the issue is not copying the Japanese directly but in reblending our mixture of objectives and constraints. I, for one, would certainly be willing to see a little less efficiency in our capital markets in exchange for a modicum of efficiency in our labor markets.

To some extent the different efficiency objectives spring from the much discussed difference in time horizons between Japanese and U.S. managers. In Japan long-run success is believed to flow from the ability to mobilize human capital, not financial capital. Thus it is more important to conserve and improve the human base than the capital base.

Many American managers would agree with that judgment but argue that they have no choice but to focus on short-term financial objectives. In America a failure to raise quarterly profits regularly will lead to a low price-earnings multiple on the stock exchanges and the dangers of a takeover bid. Realistic American managers know that in most takeover bids, the incumbent managers lose their jobs within a short period of time. By contrast, the Japanese banking institutions prevent unfriendly corporate takeovers. Having more of an investment banking relationship with their clients, Japanese banks have direct access to management and could see that managers were replaced if they so desired. They do not rely on outsiders to make management changes, and they own enough stock to prevent outsiders from proceeding with any takeover bid without their cooperation.

American managers typically receive large bonuses based on the current profits generated in their particular profit center. An American company president who makes a large fraction of his or her lifetime income based on the bonuses earned while president will be primarily interested in maximizing profits during his term of office. To do otherwise would be surprising. Japanese bonuses are not as large and depend on the outcome of the entire company, not one particular part of it. Everyone—not just the managers—gets bonuses. Japanese managers know that their entire career will depend on the long-run success of their company because they will never be able to leave their current employer. American managers know that good short-run divisional profits can lead to lucrative opportunities for moving to new companies.

The different patterns lead to different strengths and weaknesses. The advantages are not all on one side. When it comes to promoting economic growth, the advantages seem to lie with the Japanese. Their labor force is more cooperative, more willing to acquire new skills and to employ new technologies, and more interested in discovering productivity-enhancing improvements. The Japanese system may, however, prove to be fragile when coping with long-term economic slowdowns. How can they cut costs and stop from going broke in a system with lifetime employment? Will people be willing to take the necessary cutbacks if zero economic growth goes on for very long? Harmony is much easier in a high-growth economy than it is in a low-growth economy. Dividing a growing economic pie is much easier than cutting a declining pie. No one knows exactly how well the Japanese economy will cope with recessions, since the Japanese economy was so small and so good at exporting that, in previous world recessions, it was able to sail along with a temporary slowdown at most. But Japan is now so big and world economic downturns so severe and lengthy that it is not possible for Japan to continue growing if the rest of the world stops.

Because of Japan's success its position in the world economy is changing, and those changes will force alterations in some of the practices that have made Japan a success. For decades the Japanese capital market has been segregated from that of the rest of the world. In early 1982 Japanese interest rates were only one-third of those in the United States. This could happen only if something, or someone, was preventing funds from flowing out of Japan to take advantage of higher American interest rates. In contrast, Europeans with their open capital markets quickly found that they were forced to pay American interest rates.

As Shoichi Royama describes it, Japan, formerly an isolated capital market where governmental credit institutions and large financial firms managed (directed) capital flows, is shifting to become part of an international capital market where funds will flow in accordance with market incentives. The sources of government control over the capital markets are disappearing. Where firms once earned few profits, many now have substantial internal savings. Where firms once depended on Japanese banks, they can now borrow from international banks. Where foreign exchange was once scarce and rationed, it is now abundant and unrationed. Where the world was once willing to tolerate a closed Japanese capital market while welcoming the Japanese to participate in their own capital markets, it is no longer willing to do so.

A shift to open capital markets has consequences that will require changes in other parts of the Japanese economy. With open capital markets Japan would have had America's 19 percent prime lending rate in 1981. Instead of growing as it did in 1981, the Japanese economy would have been falling with such an interest rate. Part of the bargain between Japanese industry and government has been a government promise to prevent recessions. With an open capital market, world recessions will more quickly become Japanese recessions. What happens to government-business cooperation if government cannot keep its half of the bargain?

As technology and economic events force changes on our societies, so change is inevitably forced on the corporation. How does the Japanese corporation cope with economic change? How are its strategies determined? This is the topic of Ichiro Hattori of the Seiko Corporation. In his discussion of Seiko's strategic planning, Hattori mentions that Seiko's target rate of return is 7.5 percent. This should lead to an implication that has not yet sunk in among American managers. In a genuinely competitive world where no one has a large technological lead, those who are willing to do more work for less force everyone else to adapt to their standards. Competition is an environment where workers and firms are forced to change habits to remain competitive.

It has become commonplace in the American business community, for example, to note that if Japanese automobile productivity is equal to that of the United States, then American auto workers are going to have to be willing to work for the $13 per hour paid to Japanese auto workers rather than the $19 per hour (including fringe benefits) Americans now get. True. But it is equally true that if Seiko is aiming for a 7.5 percent rate of return, no one who competes with them can long demand more.

Americans often point to the fact that Japanese corporations typically make a lower rate of return than their American counterparts and act as if that proves something is wrong with the Japanese. They just as regularly fail to remark on the obvious implication. If American firms are to compete with Japanese firms, then the demanded American rate of return on sales or investment will have to fall for the American corporation just as the demanded wage will have to fall for the American auto worker. Both are necessary if American firms are to compete. The days of high rates of return are over. They were the by-product of a huge technological lead that is not there any more.

While the world is becoming competitive, America is also becoming fully integrated for the first time in the world economy. In 1971 America exported 6 percent of its GNP, but by 1981, 13 percent of the GNP was being exported— not far below the 17 percent exported from Japan. America is almost as dependent on international trade as is Japan. The only difference is that they know it and we do not. Given the growing dependence of America on international trade and a history of paying little attention to international markets, perhaps Americans have more to learn in the area of exporting to foreign markets than in any other. Takashi Kiuchi, a general manager from the international operations group at Mitsubishi Electric, describes his firm's strategic approach to international markets and how it would like to become a genuinely international firm such as Royal Dutch Shell rather than simply a Japanese exporter. But to do so, major changes, such as learning how to integrate non-Japanese managers into a Japanese corporation, must be made.

Mention international trade and the great trading companies and their associated industrial groupings—Mitsui, Mitsubishi, Sumatomo, Fuji—come immediately to mind. What is the role of these groups and their trading companies? How do they affect competition and cooperation among the big firms in Japan? Munemichi Inoue, manager of economic research at the Marubeni Trading Corporation, brings an insider's view.

In many ways the voluntary and involuntary changes forced on the Japanese are the reverse of those forced on us. One can tell a tale of historical convergence. In response to external and internal pressures, or opportunities, Japan is moving, slowly but surely, from a highly structured economy led by government toward a more market-oriented economy. This does not mean that government will play no role in the new structure but that it will play a different role. It might play less of a role in credit allocation and more of a role in directing expenditures on research and development.

Conversely, the American economy is gradually changing some of its traditional structures in response to opportunities and failures. To some extent future presidential campaigns will revolve around the issue of whether the United States should have industrial policies. This will be true regardless of whom the Democrats or Republicans nominate. The Democrats will be for industrial policies, the Republicans against them. The impetus for this debate springs from a simple set of observations.

In the 1950s Japan announced that it was going to conquer the shipbuilding industry. Industry and government resources were mobilized to this end. The shipbuilding industry was conquered. Later the same announcements and mobilization were directed toward the steel industry, with the same success. Consumer electronics followed. Now the announced intention is to conquer the knowledge industries. Given the record of success, the rest of the world fears that a similar record of success is in the offing.

The essay on industrial policies by Toshimasa Tsuruta reminds us that the auto industry also conquered the world, but without the help of ever being a targeted sunrise industry. Perhaps the Japanese success had nothing to do with targeted industries but depends on some other factor. Whatever their role in the past, Tsuruta sees industrial policies and the Ministry of International Trade and Industry (MITI) playing a smaller role in the economy tomorrow than they played yesterday. Given that MITI played its most prominent role in the recovery of the Japanese economy from the devastation of World War II, it is clear that whatever the role for industrial policies, American industrial policies cannot copy what the Japanese did in the past. The real question is whether we could take a general approach, industrial policies, from the Japanese and turn it into something that could work in America in the 1980s. This is not a question that can be answered from the Japanese experience, but the Japanese experience can shed some light on the answer.

Industrial policies are not just a matter of sunrise industries or new research and development efforts, such as the fifth-generation computer project or the very-large-scale integrated circuits project. There is also, in the words of Saburo Okita, the matter of an orderly retreat in the sunset areas of the economy. Recession cartels are used to speed up and consolidate change in declining industries. Can America learn to engineer orderly retreats, or must it simply endure periodic routs, such as that now going on in steel, imposed by the market? Munemichi Inoue asks what is an unanswered question in the American context. "Who is watching out for the steel industry and worrying about how to make it viable?" No one? The market?

Perhaps some potential answers are visible in Okita's description of what has happened in the Japanese economy since World War II and why it came about. Or in Hisao Kanamori's (a former deputy director of the Economic Planning Agency and now head of the Japan Economic Research Center) forecast of the opportunities and prospects for the Japanese economy in the future, Can the economic miracle continue? Will Japan remain the world's leader in economic growth? What lessons can we all learn?

Clearly there is no one answer to be learned from Japanese management or the Japanese economy. Trading companies have just been made legal in the United States. They are not a magic answer to the American problem but perhaps can help us improve on our exporting performance. Antitrust laws that permit General Motors and Toyota to discuss the joint production of cars while prohibiting General Motors and Ford from having the same discussion would seem to be out of date. They ought to be changed. Cooperative government-business research and development projects such as the fifth-generation computer project are not cure-alls, but perhaps we are no longer rich enough to force five different firms to invent the same wheel. Perhaps government has to become more closely linked to civilian industrial research.

To help in this effort, at the end of each chapter I provide a short essay analyzing some of the implications that the chapter raises for the reblending of the American economic mixture. In each case the aim is not to copy what the Japanese are doing but to use their experience as a source of new ideas for improving the inputs into the American blend of economic practices and institutions.

1

Motivation and Productivity

Hiroshi Takeuchi

Japanese business organizations paradoxically use the principle of equality to motivate employees to compete and simultaneously to cooperate with one another.

There is in fact hardly any difference in starting salary between newly recruited blue- and white-collar workers. For instance, the pay for senior high school graduates who have served in the same company for four years is almost the same as the starting salary for newly recruited university graduates (who are all paid equally). And often the starting salaries for graduates with advanced degrees are lower than the salaries of university graduates with bachelor's degrees who have served in the company for two to five years.

In some companies salary differentials may expand for employees who have served for more than ten years and widen over time with the success or failure of the firms. But differentials among employees of such companies are smaller, far smaller than those in other countries. The pretax income of the president of a leading Japanese company is four to five times more than that of the average blue-collar worker of his age and even smaller once progressive taxes are taken into account.

To illustrate the system, let us suppose that thirty persons are recruited in the same year. One or two of them are rated low in their annual efficiency reviews. They are paid less than others and lag behind others in promotion. But the few who receive exceptionally high ratings are not paid extra. For it is felt that the promotion of only one or two persons will cause the remaining twenty-odd employees to lose their will to work. If only one or two persons are rated low, the remaining employees will be encouraged to work.

For those who have failed, there is even a consolation system. Even those who are slow to be promoted can catch up with others if their performances improve. Employees compete keenly with each other because of the principle of equal treatment and not for fear of falling off what Americans call "the fast track."

Job rotation for all employees is also an important component of labor management. Newly employed workers fresh from school start their careers with humble jobs, such as tellers in banks and ticket punchers in railroad companies. Even engineering graduates are required to do clerical work at the head office, and those recruited for clerical jobs work in the factory. Since Japanese universities do not teach practical knowledge, job rotation serves as an in-house and on-the-job training system for all new business recruits.

The same process occurs with blue-collar workers. A new recruit handling a small lathe will later on be assigned to other machines, such as a medium- or large-sized lathe, then a milling cutter, and, over several years, to the installation of machine tools. In this way blue-collar workers are trained to handle all sorts of machines and even manage a factory. All employees experience different jobs, understand relations between different posts, and come to see the interests of the company as a whole. Despite the high costs of such transfers businesses carry them out because they believe that in the long run, benefits exceed the short-run costs.

Japanese businesses start with the belief that all people have about the same ability. Let us suppose that a Mr. Suzuki has developed an innovative technology. Other employees of the firm recognize his achievement, but this does not necessarily mean that they assess his ability particularly highly. They will probably say: "Messrs. Sato, Yamada, and others worked hard at the factory and earned profits to provide ample funds for Mr. Suzuki's research work. If Messrs. Sato, Yamada, and others had been assigned to the same job as Mr. Suzuki, they would have produced the same achievement. They were engaged in harder and thankless work instead." Suzuki was able to develop the technology because of the efforts of many other researchers working under him and also because of research work undertaken by his seniors and fellow workers. It is usually judged that Suzuki was able to produce the achievement with the support of the entire staff including the blue-collar workers, not by his ability alone. The credit should go not to Suzuki but to the personnel department, which assigned him to the laboratory, and also to the head of the laboratory who gave the research project to him. Therefore his achievement belongs to the company, not to himself, and therefore he is not a special person.

If Suzuki concludes that his achievement was made possible by his ability alone and openly says so, he will provoke antipathy from all other workers and will be unable to stay in the firm. Another company will not employ him, however talented he may be, because he cannot cooperate with others. Major businesses will probably worry that employing such a person will sour their relations with his former employers. And even if Suzuki wants to go into business on his own account, his old company would not cooperate with him, and no other researchers would help him. Therefore Suzuki would be better off concluding not that he has an outstanding ability but that other people are equally capable and that he was simply fortunate to get that job.

Thus the principle of equality prevails in business. Few are chosen for special promotion; there can be no heroes and elite employees. Most people are promoted simultaneously through the same route, and some people are dropped from the race each year. But the dropouts can enter the race again in several years. Equality and competition coexist in the system for everyone.

Japanese practice contrasts with Western business in many other respects. In the United States, for instance, there are detailed manuals for most jobs, and any person who reads a manual can understand the nature and process of the work concerned. Such manuals tell workers with whom they should consult in case of trouble. Jobs are extremely simplified. In construction work, for example, pipes are classified by color, and workers on the construction site simply connect pipes of the same color. In Japanese enterprises, manuals, if there are any, are not so detailed, and usually there are none for clerical work. If jobs are extremely simple and employees are assigned to work mechanically as in manuals, many of them will probably feel offended for being treated like children.

If employers set loose limits to work and leave details to the discretion of the workers, employees will feel encouraged to work on their own initiative and develop themselves in the company. As an example, consider A, who is motivated but not so competent. If B, who is particularly good at his work, finishes his job quickly and helps A, in time B will gain the confidence of his fellow workers because of his outstanding performance and his contribution.

The main goal of personnel management is to confirm the confidence of fellow workers in each other. If an employee makes a mistake, the supervisor is unlucky. He cannot sacrifice his subordinates, with whom he has worked for many years. Instead he defends the person, and his colleagues and superiors will not call him to account too hard because they know that he is unlucky. Thus the question of responsibility for the mistake is left unpursued. In business corporations it is considered a virtue for workers to protect each other as if the others were family members.

An organization that trusts its employees and entrusts work to them has no need for supervisors. In Western businesses the elite supervise and instruct the workers. They report for work early, work until late at night, and often work weekends. In Japan executives report for work late in the morning, read the newspaper first, meet many guests, and leave the office early in the evening. Regular employees must work overtime, but they feel they work even more efficiently after their superiors leave because they do not like to be given detailed instructions. In Western countries executives shut themselves up in their offices, work with the help of their own secretaries, and issue instructions. Japanese executives have their own offices, but the offices are used for receiving visitors; the executives work with their subordinates in the same large office. They observe progress in the work entrusted to their subordinates, sense problems, and give advice in such a way as not to discourage their subordinates' will to work.

Salaried workers in Japan have a saying: "Be controversial in your twenties, but after you have passed your fortieth-year milestone, lose the argument." In other words, young employees should argue aggressively with others to develop an understanding of work, but by the time they are senior managers, winning an argument with subordinates only discourages the subordinates' will to work. Deliberately losing an argument to subordinates encourages their will to work and thus benefits the company.

In Japan the most important task for supervisors is to forge a team among subordinates and help develop their confidence and abilities. If a competent subsection chief works hard, his section chief is well regarded for having trained him, and the section chief's position rises. Therefore section chiefs readily teach subsection chiefs how to handle work, who in turn eagerly teach it to their subordinates. No section chiefs refuse to teach subsection chiefs how to handle jobs for fear that they will lose their posts to capable subsection chiefs or that the subsection chief will be promoted over them. It simply isn't going to happen. Any manager who acted in such an antisocial way would be disqualified to hold a supervisory post and would be assigned work that could be performed alone.

Because Japanese corporations regard all newly recruited employees as having the same ability and think that their abilities can be equally developed while serving in various capacities, they use length of service—seniority—as the basis for order and pay. Therefore seniors are usually expected to give instructions to juniors. Conversely, young persons, however capable, cannot instruct elders in handling work.

Although seniors lose physical strength and mental capacity as they grow old, in Japanese corporations the decline of mental capacity and the growth of the right of command, which seem to contradict each other, are fully compatible. Consider the life cycle of a salaried worker. In his twenties and thirties he works very hard to perform the work entrusted to him. In his late thirties he assumes a supervisory post, and his hard-working young subordinates more than make up for the decline in his mental capacity. In most cases seniors simply guide young workers in the right direction while yielding arguments to them. But being the most senior in his section, only he has the right to issue orders, and an important task for him is to make decisions and give proper orders.

Although his mental capacity declines in his forties and fifties, he nevertheless has acquired an acute power of recognizing and soliciting the opinions of others. He also has become a good judge of character and acquired the business acumen that enables him to make sound decisions. He may give a key post to A who is prudent when passive management is needed in a recession. When aggressive management is needed in prosperous times, he will replace

A with B, who is aggressive. An elderly person acquires such power of observation and diplomacy only with experience.

Thoughtful consideration of others is needed in business management and of course can be expected of those versed in the ways of the Japanese people. Old people provide the knowledge on the conduct of ceremonies of coming of age, marriage, funeral, and ancestral worship and on the proper way to make gifts. Thus there is a strong sense of unity among the elderly, middle-aged, and young, and this social bond is carried over to employees in Japanese corporations. In this respect the Japanese seniority system is a product of a social climate that evolved over several hundred years.

In Japanese corporations, when the most senior person gives an order, the person next in rank, acting on the order, issues a new order which is passed down from one person to another. The person in the highest post may simply issue orders in abstract terms, such as telling his staff to raise the technical level or overcome a management crisis. The order becomes more specific as it is passed down, and the whole company starts moving toward the target. In Japan the system of entrusting work to subordinates to encourage their will to work and increase productivity has been used for several hundred years. Nobuhiro Sato, an eighteenth-century economist, wrote that managers should have employees well in hand and entrust work to them. The merchant families in the Tokugawa era held similar precepts.

In Western countries the elite among employees are singled out at the time of their employment according to educational background and other qualifications. In Japan all are treated equally at the time of employment, and they climb the ladder of seniority in a group, with low achievers given opportunities to become high achievers and to catch up with early starters, thus encouraging employees' will to work. In their late forties, however, they begin to diverge.

Some are promoted to top management posts while others can expect to rise to no more than department or section chiefs. Thus the principle of equality applies to those who have not yet reached middle age. They compete while being treated equally, and candidates for top management posts are chosen through the competition. Remember also that the average worker spends his whole career in the same firm. Being promoted gradually under the rotation system, he may become the chairman of the union of employees and return to regular work when his term as the union leader ends and, if fortunate, he may be promoted to a top management post. The dividing line between workers and managers is not very rigid.

Japanese companies treat employees as if they were family members. An employee who becomes crippled from an automobile accident after several years of service with the firm will continue to be employed and will not be discharged even if his work efficiency has fallen. If he dies in an automobile accident and his wife and children are unable to make a living, his company will probably give his wife an office job, hire her as a caretaker of a company dormitory for unmarried employees, or give her a job with a company-operated recreation facility. It will probably lend money interest free to pay for his children's school expenses.

Even a company in financial difficulty will not lay off employees unless it is on the verge of bankruptcy. If it suffers a loss, its president will cut his own pay; if he cuts his by half, the pay for other executives will be cut by 40 percent and that for middle-level management by 20 percent. Only after the firm's performance has failed to improve despite the pay cuts will it cut the pay for rank and file. As a last resource, if all these measures fail, the firm will lay off employees. And when the president decides on a personnel reduction, he must be prepared to resign.

In Japan company presidents pay greater attention to employees than to stockholders. Since employees spend their working life in the same company, they cannot leave the company even if they do not like it. Stockholders simply hold shares in it. Stockholders have various opinions in managing the shares they hold in a company; they expect their value to rise or to receive steady dividends. If stockholders conclude that the company has no bright future, they will sell their shares. If the company is taking a wrong course, employees will do their best to urge it to change policy, but they must continue to serve in the company until they reach retirement age. Thus both management and labor work in the interests of fellow company employees and not for stockholders.

When in a poll presidents of leading companies were asked: "As the chief executive, for whom are you responsible?" 85 percent of the respondents answered "the employees." Although Japanese joint-stock enterprises are similar in structure to their Western counterparts, they still epitomize a very Japanese view. The employees are bound together as trusted comrades, not merely by the pursuit of financial interests.

In large part this trust stems from the fact that Japanese people know their roles in work. Even a person holding a high position will not make a decision independently. First, he must order his subordinates or organization to study a matter and consider the conclusion reached before he makes a decision. If the president makes decisions by himself all the time on his own authority, he will soon lose the support of his subordinates and become unable to exercise his ability. His subordinates will feel hurt, turn their backs on him, and, in effect, ignore his orders, although they may pretend to obey them.

When a government agency is going to make a major policy decision, the matter is studied first by the section in charge, the smallest unit of the organization, and the internal bureaus and other departments discuss the conclusion drawn by the section and coordinate their views and then refine it at higher levels.

Major questions are referred to councils for deliberation; a council will listen to the views of interested persons of learning and experience to reach a consensus. Council members who strongly dissent may attempt to ruin the proposed plan by persuasively arguing against it. To prevent the plan from being killed, government officials in charge of it must assume a low profile, provide data to council members, listen carefully to their opinions, and draw the kind of conclusion the agency wants. In this process the draft policy proposed by the section in charge is modified at various levels and obtains the support of not only the internal bureaus but also persons of learning and experience in private enterprises.

Persons serving on such councils include representatives of newspapers, consumer organizations, and labor unions so that public opinion will not be hostile to it. Sometimes the government briefs reporters on policy decisions to gauge public reaction. In this way promoters lay the groundwork for a consensus on an important policy among the parties concerned.

Such a groundwork is also indispensable in decision making by private corporations. This practice is one reason why foreigners complain that Japanese businesses take too much time to make decisions. This groundwork is a mechanism that involves everyone in the process of decision making, and they derive the will to work from it.

Japanese tend to define themselves by their work. When people are asked, "Who are you?" almost all will give their names and the names of their companies or organizations. Even a university professor will probably answer, "I am a professor at the University of Tokyo," instead of "I am an economist." Almost all people consider themselves members of corporate society and fulfill themselves through their companies.

Being members of a corporate society, employees work overtime for their companies, sacrificing their personal affairs when necessary. When business earnings are poor, they are content with small wage increases because they know that if their companies fail to achieve sustained growth due to high wages, their incomes will fall in the long run.

The difference between the corporate sense of Japanese and Western employees and businesses can be seen in their experience with the introduction of robots. Japan uses more industrial robots than all other countries combined. Most of these robots were developed not by robot makers but by users, such as automakers and transport companies, who wanted to minimize heavy labor. The robots are used for the simplest jobs, and nobody fears that they will lose their jobs. Instead, workers quickly rise in the organization, and they feel relieved that they are no longer required to do dirty work. Factory workers handling industrial robots give them pet names and regard them as subordinates. They believe that the robots help increase productivity, which will result in increasing their wages and contribute to the growth of their company, from which they can derive a sense of pride.

I believe that the productivity of the Japanese economy has been so high because of the delicate sense of balance inherent in the Japanese people. Employees compete with one another while cooperating among themselves. The president and others holding supervisory posts listen to the opinions of their subordinates and take these positions into consideration when giving orders. High Japanese productivity seems closely related to those relationships.

The Japanese sense of morality is based on long traditions, and Japanese business organizations are based on such traditional senses of morality.

Lester Thurow
Reblending the American Economic Mixture

Teamwork versus the individual: Both are essential to a well-functioning economic organization, but what is the right mixture? Clearly the Japanese structure puts more emphasis on creating good teamwork, whereas the American structure puts more emphasis on encouraging the brilliant individual.

New American business school graduates work hard to get on the fast track early in their careers; in Japan the fast track does not start until a manager is in his forties. As Takeuchi mentions, the difference between the Western and Japanese practices is whether employees are distinguished at the beginning or the end. If everyone knows who the economic winners are within the first five years of joining the firm, then 95 percent of the labor force will psychologically give up and let the 5 percent carry the load of making the firm productive. But 5 percent of the labor force can never make an efficient team. In Japan where employees do not know who the 5 percent will be until twenty or twenty-five years into their career, individuals will work harder longer to put themselves into that elite 5 percent.

Part of the reason for the widely commented on differences in managerial time horizons must come about from the employment structure. In the United States a manager gets on the fast track by suggesting something that leads to an immediate payoff in profits. In Japan the real payoff is to those who make suggestions that lead to visible success twenty to twenty-five years later. This is reinforced by one's inability to leave one's original company to join another. Personal success is tied to the success of one's corporation in a way that is not true in the United States since it is not possible to bail out of a losing company and become a successful manager elsewhere. As a result a corporate failure is much more serious to individuals in Japan than it is in the United States.

The seniority pay system where education does not affect starting wages also leads to a very different mixture of skills within the firm. Consider engineers. On a per capita basis Japan produces twice as many engineers as does the United States, and as a consequence the average firm will have twice as many engineers on its payrolls as its American counterpart. Is it any surprise that under this circumstance Japanese products are a little bit better engineered than American products? Yet American firms would not want or be able to hire twice as many engineers given the high wages that must be paid to new engineers relative to the wages of the average worker.

In the United States talented engineers also bail out of engineering and into management long before they burn out as talented engineers. They do not want to miss the pay and promotions of being on the fast track. But individual rationality leads to social irrationality; individuals do not fully utilize their scientific education. That could, however, easily be prevented if individuals were able to catch the fast track express at a later point in their careers.

It is impossible for America to copy the Japanese system of pay and employment. But the Japanese system tells us that we should reblend our incentives, putting more emphasis on creating a good team and less emphasis on letting brilliant individuals get to the top instantly. Must teamwork be a lost art in the United States?

2

The Impact of Japanese Culture on Management

Masakazu Yamazaki

At the end of the Edo period in the late nineteenth century, Japan undertook to study Western management and industry. It did not take up the subject of effective management by itself, however, but attempted to understand Western culture: Western education, Western history, and Western ways of thinking. It tried to assimilate the Western philosophy of individualism and human rights. The art and literature of the West met with overwhelming enthusiasm.

As a consequence a large number of Japanese came to regard French literature or English and American literature as *the* literature. English is taught to all Japanese children when they enter junior high school. When Tokyo University opened its faculties of management and economics, it had already had a faculty of literature where cultural and social sciences were taught in the Western way. Students were sent abroad with the saying, "When you want to buy clothes, you must also buy a wardrobe to put them in."

Has accepting Western culture changed Japanese society? The answer is yes. But has it completely westernized

Japanese society? The answer is no. The result has been a unique form of pluralism in our cultural system, in our sense of values, and even in our style of living. This cultural pluralism is one of the notable characteristics shared by Japan and Western countries.

In the seventeenth century Western intellectuals took an adventurous step and introduced Arabian science into their Christian culture. And we can find in Shakespeare knowledge of Greek myths mixed with Christian faith.

There is, however, a decisive difference between Western pluralism and that pluralism which played a big part in the modernization of Japan in the Meiji period. In the West pluralism resulted in an attempt to integrate all of the various elements into one whole. In Japan various elements formed close relationships with one another while keeping their independence.

In the West cultural pluralism is found between relatively homogeneous beliefs. In religion, for instance, various sects coexist under one and the same principle—the God of Christianity. Catholics and Protestants exist side by side and engage in what has often been intense competition.

In Japan pluralism takes the form of ties between heterogeneous units. Christianity can be found alongside Buddhism and Shintoism, but this coexistence has produced no competition.

Another characteristic of Japanese pluralism is that it is lodged in the minds of single individuals or within their personal styles of living rather than in different social groups. Different tastes, thoughts, and manners of living can coexist within one person. People adopt different sensibilities on various occasions in their lives.

For example, a great number of newspapers and weekly magazines are published in Japan today, some of them highbrow and others not. This is no different from the United States. But these different publications are not characterized by social class. They are read on different occasions. It is no exaggeration to say that one person may read a first-rate daily at home, a financial paper in his office, and on the train to and from his work, a weekly magazine full of gossip and pornography. Western newspapers are clearly associated with specific social classes, and one individual is not often seen reading different types of publications on different occasions.

Cultural pluralism of this kind could be found in Japan even in ancient days. Over the past thousand years there has been a complex intermingling of Chinese, Indian, and Korean elements. For example, Japan took in ideographs from China, Buddhism from India, and outstanding art and porcelain from Korea. And on top of these foreign influences we managed to create our own literature, tea ceremony, and other cultural phenomena.

Since Japan was an island country, surrounded by the sea, and secure from invasions by foreign powers, it was able to accept and assimilate foreign or heterogeneous tastes and thoughts without undue anxiety about foreign domination. On the other hand, Japan was also not strong enough or did not have enough ambition to cross the sea and invade other countries or peoples of other faiths.

If it had tried to conquer and convert pagans, an integrated ideology would have been necessary. But since there was no necessity to overcome another culture, Japan did not feel the need to solidify its own culture as one homogeneous and unshakable entity.

This cultural pluralism led to the emergence of a unique kind of philosophy, which we may call "agnosticism without nihilism." The Japanese have always taken the position that they do not know whether there is an ultimate, immovable, one and only truth. But they harbor a sense of profound awe toward a transcendental being and will not denigrate another person's belief different from theirs.

This agnosticism without nihilism has led to a kind of pragmatism. To put it differently, it is rationalism based on the process of trial and error. We have always taken the attitude that we do not know what kind of systematic structure the world has or what ultimate truth that systematic structure is based on, but we do pay sufficient attention to the understanding of each objective fact so that we can see how that fact is rationally related to others.

I recall an interesting episode. Toyotomi Hideyoshi, who ruled Japan in the sixteenth century, was presented with a map of the world by a Christian missionary. He had this atlas copied on a *byobu* screen. This screen still exists, and when we look at it, we find that although the entire map is very faithfully copied, it has no lines to indicate longitude and latitude. At that time Japanese sailors went to China mainly by sailing along the coast. They needed precise knowledge about the courses connecting one port with another, but they did not have to know by means of longitude and latitude where the center of the world was or how their present position was related to it, this like the agnosticism without nihilism that brought forth tolerance toward all kinds of thoughts and beliefs.

The Japanese are reluctant to believe any unitary view of the world thoroughly. This manifests itself in two typical forms. One is the idea that the world is constantly changing, and everything will move on like a flowing river. We call this the sense of transitoriness—an idea enhanced by the Buddhist view of the world. The other is the Japanese habit of taking an ironical attitude toward any sort of dogma or truth. It is the attitude of believing in something and yet not believing it completely. It is the conviction that all truths harbor their opposite truths inside them.

These two Japanese ideas can be found in Western culture. Certainly the idea that all truths contain their opposites within them can be found in Shakespeare. At the beginning of *Macbeth,* the witches cry out, "Fair is foul and foul is fair."

But when the two attitudes are united, however, they produce a very Japanese and distinctive view of life. The Japanese take an ironical attitude even about their own sense of transitoriness in this world. Although the Japanese see the world as transitory, they neither take an unrealistic attitude nor try to escape from the realities of the world. To the contrary, our ancestors tried to live more realistically precisely because the world was transitory.

A significant clue to this ironical sense of transitoriness is provided by the concluding paragraph of an essay, "An Account of My Hut," one of the classic pieces of prose literature of Japan written in the early thirteenth century. In this essay, noted for its typical medieval pessimism that wails over the ephemerality of worldly things, the author, Kamo no Chomei, eulogizes his ideal life in seclusion from mundane wealth and fame. After comparing man's fate to the ever-changing flow of water and the bubbles in the pool forming and vanishing without long duration, he meticulously describes his quiet living in the deep mountain with adoration. Yet he concludes this essay by adding a few lines with an unexpected note of doubt that sounds rather contradictory to all that comes before: "Now the moon of my life is slipping down the western sky, and I shall soon have to face the darkness beyond the Styx. Why should I denounce the worldly things in this manner? Since Buddha preaches us not to be attached to anything, it must be a fault and a sin for me to feel attached to my humble cottage and the quietude it affords me. Why should I thus waste time in relating such trifling pleasures of my secluded life?"

A number of works of world literature idealize life in seclusion. But it would be rare to find one in which the extolment of hermitage is followed by a confession of doubts about it. Generally, the sacred and the profane are at opposite poles. It is deemed to be an ideal in any other culture to try to detach oneself from the profane and to go straight to the sacred. Idealism should translate itself into dedicated efforts for the pure and thoroughgoing realization of a chosen value. But contrary to this commonsense view of idealism, Kamo no Chomei seems to suggest that a straight pursuit of seclusion from the profane has a self-

defeating effect of rewakening attachment to one's sub-
jective view of the world—which is itself worldly. He is
warning against the dangers of self-righteousness hidden
beneath moral fastidiousness. He seems to mean to say that
it is counterproductive, whatever the chosen value to be
realized, to pursue it singlemindedly to an extreme. Ideals
are best achieved when the pursuit is curbed in the middle
of the way.

Such an ironical view of hermitage was widespread in
medieval Japan. It was customary then for a successful
patriarch still in the prime of his life to hand over his estate
to his heir and to live as a hermit without actually moving
out of the household.

The tea ceremony as an avocation with its austere atmosphere provided successful men with a temporary hermitage that allowed them to seclude themselves from the
world without actually leaving it for good. On the other
hand, many of the great leaders of Japanese politics were
truly pessimistic yet worked out a pragmatic design for
leading an earthly life.

The Emperor Daigo, for instance, for all his yearning for
Chinese pastoral poets, engineered a golden age in the
political history of the nation. Toyotomi Hideyoshi, who
reunified the divided country within the space of his
lifetime and founded today's megalopolis of Osaka, con-
fessed on his deathbed that "the business of Osaka is just a
dream within a dream." The 250 years of the Edo period
that enjoyed bustling affluence was at the same time dominated by the notion of *ukiyo,* or ephemeral world, so much
that even works of entertainment were called *ukiyo-e,
ukiyo-zoshi,* and the like.

Most Japanese are ironical pessimists. But instead of allowing their pessimism to lead them into gloom, they de-
rived a kind of healthy pragmatism from their awareness of
life's evanescence. This uniquely Japanese pessimism may
not be as obvious today as it was in premodern times, but
there is every indication that it is still a powerful under-

current in the psychology of the hard-working Japanese people. Their bias in music toward elegiac tunes in minor keys is well known, and a recent survey of popular lyrics reveals overwhelming preferences for sentimental notions of "parting company," "shedding tears," "falling leaves," and "going north." The widely acclaimed heroes of Ozu Yasujiro's movies are sound and solid citizens, who, convinced as they are in their own sense of transitoriness, go routinely and effectively about the business of daily life.

To verbalize what those pessimistic and yet diligent Japanese may assert inwardly, one could perhaps say that we have no idea about the absolute and ultimate end of our lives, but we should try to live faithfully and elaborately each and every detailed phase of life as it unfolds around us. One could also say that since we cannot choose to achieve one single task that is central and essential to the meaning of our whole life, we should pour all our energy into day-to-day business.

The wide acceptance of such a belief may be a particularly Japanese phenomenon, but the thesis itself is not the exclusive property of the Japanese. Wolfgang von Goethe, one of the great thinkers of the West, was in part an agnostic himself, and he offered the following advice for those living under the burden of agnosticism: "How can one know oneself? By deed, not by meditation. Try to fulfill your obligations, and you will at once realize what you are. What then are our obligations? Just those day-to-day things to be done."

Goethe's words had a great impact on Mori Ogai, a leading intellectual during the early stage of Japan's modernization, when he himself felt that he had known no other norm for his life than "those day-to-day things to be done." He bequeathed to his family a household motto saying, "You should be able to be engaged in trifling things as if they were really enjoyable."

Such attitudes explain a lot of Japanese phenomena that are ostensibly contradictory to each other and often seem inscrutable to foreigners. Now we can see the reason why the quiet and serene tea ceremony is compatible in the mind of the Japanese with the busy and hectic activities of modern industries. This also sheds light on the contrast between their fastidious perfectionism in technology and the rather loosely systematized urban design of their big cities. Above all it provides an explanation to the fact that average Japanese are strongly loyal to their intimate social groups, such as their families, business firms, or country villages, and are less interested in their nation as a whole or the international community. To them, these small units of society are the only part of the generally unknowable world of which they can at least be sure. And perhaps it seems irresponsible and presumptuous to them to talk too much about the vast universe beyond those small territories.

In this connection one must recall that the Japanese traditionally call their business or profession *michi* ("the way"), a word with strong religious overtones in the Japanese language. *Michi* stands for not only a technical means necessary for one's job but also implies the way by which one can know oneself, not through wisdom but through deed. Workers, farmers, and craftsmen have been encouraged always to stick to their own place of work. They have been convinced that it is the only way for them to learn who they are. This tradition is still preserved to some extent in the minds of employees of today's business firms and contributes to the concept of lifetime employment.

This unique agnosticism of the Japanese has nothing to do with nihilism or skepticism in the negative sense. Their ironical attitude to any kind of monistic view of the world represents neither a cynicism about ideals nor an eclecticism that tends to distort ideals. It is instead based on their healthy pluralistic view of the world, a view that there may be more than one single perspective by which one can grasp and interpret what this world really is.

It is too early at this moment of history to judge whether this Japanese understanding of the world can offer any useful lesson to the non-Japanese community, but it may be worthwhile for all of us to remind ourselves that every nation is becoming more and more similar to that of pre-modern Japan. In the complicated equilibrium of the big powers, every nation is today relatively strong enough to resist invasions by foreign powers. This means that any culture is now safe and secure enough to be able to accept foreign or heterogeneous tastes and thoughts without undue anxiety.

By the same token, no power in the present world is now strong enough to conquer and convert "pagans" to its own ideology. This suggests that any country can now dispense with an integrated ideology or a solid homogeneous way of life. Any country can now accept some of the Japanese lessons if it wishes to do so.

Lester Thurow
Reblending the American Economic Mixture

To change institutions or practices, it is necessary in most cases to change the attitudes of the people involved. And usually this change in attitudes is of more lasting importance than any specific change in practices. Yamazaki reminds us that when Japan rapidly adopted Chinese practices in the seventh to eleventh centuries and Western practices in the nineteenth and twentieth centuries, it did not do so by narrowly studying management or science but by attempting to study the entire culture. In a similar manner part of the necessary American reblending extends far beyond that of specific economic practices.

When Yamasaki talks about agnosticism without nihilism, he is talking about being open to change and new experience without being locked into a specific framework that knows what is "true." Despite the fact that we Americans like to think of ourselves as pragmatic, we may have become, and to some extent always have been, a nation of ideologues and crusaders. From the puritans to prohibition we have tried to force moral codes on each other.

The crusading attitude can be seen in our recent debates on what role government should play in our economy. The 1980 American presidential election was won by a man arguing that government in and of itself was bad. "Get the government off the backs of the people and out of the economy." No other industrial society has a serious well-financed Committee for a Union Free Environment devoted to driving labor unions out of society. A comparison of the environmental movements in Japan and the United States shows the absence of crusaders on both sides in Japan and nothing but crusaders on both sides in the United States. Crusaders have virtues, but they resist change and cannot adjust to new conditions or new evidence.

Linked with our crusading attitude is a yearning for a golden economic past of virtue and prosperity that really never existed. Recessions, depressions, and inflation were rampant before the New Deal of the 1930s and government's involvement in the economy. The Great Depression began before government played any significant role in the economy.

From the management perspective the issue is to what extent our attitudes about the "right" way so dominate our thinking that we are unable to see, or adopt, new and more productive ways. The "right" American way is for managers to make decisions on new machinery and for the workers who are actually to be running the machines to be completely excluded from the selection of those machines. But if being able to participate in such decisions leads to a labor force more willing to cooperate and better motivated for work, the "right" way may be the "wrong" way. By adhering to the "right" way, we stop ourselves from adopting a more efficient way.

As Yamasaki notes, one of the reasons that Japanese workers are more interested in their work group is that they hold on to their group relations for individual support rather than rely on abstract ideological beliefs for individual support. While we have always been a nation of crusaders, perhaps we have become more so in recent years and need to reduce some of the crusading element in the American mixture.

3

The Perceptions and the Reality of Japanese Industrial Relations

Haruo Shimada

According to a widely prevalent stereotypic image of Japanese industrial relations in the Western world, the Japanese are a homogeneous and consensual people with industrial relations that are as a consequence harmonious, trustful, and peaceful. And so industrial relations are highly productive in Japan—as demonstrated by the remarkably successful performance of Japanese industries.

This chapter attempts to correct exaggerations and misunderstandings associated with such a stereotyped image and provide an alternative explanation of the role of industrial relations in the process of Japanese industrial growth.

The Stereotyped Image of Japanese Industrial Relations

The stereotype starts by emphasizing the common social values of Japanese society, that the Japanese are so homogeneous that they share the same culture, ideologies, tastes, historical traditions, and even behavioral patterns. This leads to *harmony, groupism,* and *consensus.* These Japanese social characteristics in turn are used to explain the unique nature of Japanese industrial relations.

Stereotypes of Western industrial relations are by contrast characterized by adversarial labor-management relations instead of harmony, individualism instead of groupism, and conflicts instead of consensus.

There are further to be considered three conspicuous institutional components of the Japanese industrial relations system. First, workers are employed for life within a particular company and are not dismissed even when the level of business activity declines, unless the decline is so deep that the company faces bankruptcy. Inherent in this notion is the worker's attitude: workers commit themselves to the company for their lifetime in return for lifetime employment. Second, a length-of-service reward system is observed by every company whereby salary levels are determined in accordance with the worker's length of service within the company. Third, in enterprise unionism a union is organized within the realm of an individual enterprise covering both white- and blue-collar workers. Such unions are consequently docile and cooperative with management.

Characterized by these three institutional components, Japanese industrial relations are thought to be unique, although to the eyes of some westerners they appear to be economically irrational. Japanese labor analysts often reinforce this impression of uniqueness. These analysts assert that the Japanese company retains its employees despite business fluctuations because it is governed more strongly by the principle of group cohesiveness than profit maximization, that the Japanese company can enjoy industrial peace with a docile enterprise union as a bargaining counterpart because both management and labor desire harmony and share common goals and interests arising out of their homogeneous natures, that the length-of-service reward system serves as an important function of social ordering within a Japanese company.

In what way and under what conditions did such perceptions become the standard stereotype of Japanese industrial relations? During the 1950s when the Japanese economy was recovering from the war, Japanese scholars regarded characteristics of Japanese industrial relations such as the length-of-service reward system and enterprise unionism as undesirable symptoms of undeveloped capitalism.

But starting in the mid-1960s, when the Japanese economy was growing rapidly, the tone of evaluation changed remarkably. An increasing number of Japanese people, including scholars, employers, and even unionists, began praising lifetime employment, the length-of-service reward system, and enterprise unionism as positive factors contributing to economic growth. Indeed, these practices were now often referred to as the "Three Sacred Treasures" of Japanese industrial relations.

In the 1960s many foreign scholars also began to pay attention to Japanese industrial relations and to conduct systematic research. They accumulated evidence and tried to make new interpretations. Some scholars pointed out that Japanese industrial relations are not as consensual or harmonious as alleged by the classical culturalists. On the basis of in-depth fieldwork in industrial plants, one sociologist revealed that beneath the seemingly harmonious groupism, there existed elements of strenuous competition, confrontation, and conflicts.

Economists provided new interpretations to the seemingly traditional employment practices by saying that those practices are in fact governed by highly rigorous economic principles of competition and optimization. They tried to explain practices of long-term employment and the length-of-service reward system as outcomes of the long process of human capital accumulation within a firm.

When more data and information were made available, other scholars expressed skepticism about the alleged uniqueness of some of the features of Japanese industrial relations. They maintained that features such as lifetime employment, earnings that increase with the length of service, and local unions are found not only in Japan but also in many other industrial countries. These interpretations commonly imply that the Japanese system is similar to other systems in terms of the functions it performs, although it may appear quite different.

Despite expert findings and interpretations that emphasize commonalities with Western practices rather than differences, it is undeniable that the popular view of Japanese industrial relations as an extension of its society still dominates. This interpretation is not surprising. Probably it reflects the fact that the performance of the Japanese economy has been outstanding among advanced industrial economies. Even if labor relations were functionally equivalent, there must remain something in the Japanese economy that explains the superior performance.

A report on industrial relations published a few years ago by the Organization for Economic Cooperation and Development (OECD) suggests that there must be a fourth pillar that makes the whole system of Japanese industrial relations work effectively. The report suggests that the fourth pillar is a unique value system commonly held by the Japanese people but leaves the real content of such a value system largely unknown.

A report on the Japanese economy published by the Brookings Institution of the United States at about the same time attributes the successful industrial performance to highly biased allocation of resources in favor of industrial production at the expense of welfare of the working class. In other words, the report stresses, in sharp contrast to the OECD report, "exploitation" and "powerless unions," which were unable to protect workers' interests. This difference in interpretation of basically the same set of observations of the Japanese economy eloquently reflects the lack of well-balanced and reliable information necessary for sound analysis.

Because of increased interest in the performance of the Japanese economy, books like *Japan as No. 1* by Ezra Vogel, *Theory Z* by William Ouchi, and *The Art of Japanese Management* by Richard Pascal and Anthony Athos gained a phenomenal popularity in both the United States and Japan. In *Theory Z,* for example, Professor Ouchi asserts that American firms do not lack capital or technology. What they lack is the human factor. He maintains that in successful business organizations, there exist "trust," "subtlety," and "intimacy,"—elements typically observed in Japanese firms and in some uniquely successful American corporations. Ouchi proposes essentially a restatement of the classical stereotype of mystic Japanese industrial relations.

Books of this type simply reinforce conventional impressions that Japanese companies enjoy a culturally unique system. They are privileged to do so because they are Japanese companies with Japanese workers.

Why does this kind of stereotype persist despite skepticism and criticisms? Again, it is basically due to a lack of well-balanced and reliable information about Japanese industrial relations.

Most foreigners visited Japan after it had entered its stage of miraculous economic growth. They studied mostly successful large business corporations in the private sector. They ignored Japanese experiences in the difficult and painstaking period preceding the era of rapid economic growth, when the crucial conditions and ground for the remarkable growth were in fact prepared. By overlooking this critical period, they failed to understand the causes responsible for triggering Japan's dynamic and successful industrial development in the subsequent period.

Also, by visiting only successful large firms, they ignored a great number of unsuccessful, unstable small firms and problematic public corporations. This bias deprived foreign observers of opportunities to investigate critical elements that generated successful cases and differentiated them from unsuccessful ones. These omissions distorted foreigners' evaluations of Japanese industries by imposing an illusion that Japanese firms are successful because they all enjoy a uniquely Japanese cultural inheritance.

To correct these misperceptions I will proceed in two steps: first, to qualify or correct misunderstandings associated with the popular image of the Three Sacred Treasures and, second, to probe for a more balanced view of the complex system of Japanese industrial relations.

Myths and the Reality of Three Sacred Treasures

I start by qualifying the concept of lifetime employment. In fact there is no lifetime employment system, in its true sense of the word, in Japan. Due to compulsory retirement, workers must leave the company of their primary employment opportunity around the age of fifty-five to sixty. Since the majority of workers retire from the labor market in their late sixties, even the most privileged workers in terms of employment security—the one-third of total employees who work for large firms—have to leave their primary employment opportunity five to ten years prior to their actual retirement.

Moreover when employment is reduced in recessions, it is these older workers who are more likely to be dismissed or sent to subsidiaries. In effect the degree of employment protection given to older workers in the Japanese employment system is much lower than that afforded American workers who can work until they reach the age eligible for full pension benefits.

Labor mobility is also not as low as one might expect from the preconception of an immobile and rigid lifetime employment system. As table 3.1 shows, 10 to 20 percent of all employees leave their firm every year. Turnover rates are higher for females than for males and higher for smaller firms than for large ones. Table 3.2 reveals that roughly

Table 3.1
Separation rates by sex and size of establishment (percent)

Size of establishment[a]	Both sexes			Male			Female		
	1970[b]	1975[c]	1980[c]	1970[b]	1975[c]	1980[c]	1970[b]	1975[c]	1980[c]
Total	21.5	15.8	14.4	16.5	11.9	10.8	30.9	23.2	20.7
1000 and over }	16.9	11.6	11.3	11.0	6.3	6.5	31.3	24.8	22.7
300–999 }	24.6	15.2	14.0	19.7	10.4	9.4	33.3	26.4	23.3
100–299		19.2	16.5		15.0	12.6		26.6	23.1
30–99	25.4	19.0	17.3	21.6	15.7	14.7	31.1	24.2	21.1
5–29	24.4	17.9	16.5	21.6	16.4	15.1	28.3	19.9	18.4

Source: Ministry of Labor, *Survey of Employment Trends.*
a. Measured in terms of number of regular employees.
b. The size classification for 1970 is 500 and more, 100 to 499, 30 to 99, and 5 to 29.
c. Figures for total include public employees.

Table 3.2
Types and composition of new entrants

Year	Total		Recent graduates	Others	Part-time workers
1965	100.0	(3.608)	31.3	21.2	47.5
1970	100.0	(4.916)	22.6	20.3	57.1
1975	100.0	(3.361)	23.3	21.3	55.4
1980	100.0	(3.812)	24.0	25.4	50.6

Source: Ministry of Labor, *Survey of Employment Trends.*
Note: Figures are for establishments with five and more employees.
They represent total number of male and female workers for all
industries except construction. Figures in parentheses are in terms
of 1,000 workers.

half of newly hired people have had an occupational experience somewhere else. Recent graduates account for
only a quarter to a third of total recruits.

These observations suggest that, quite unlike the stereotype, Japanese employment is in fact fairly flexible and
mobile. Had the Japanese labor market not had a flexible
and efficient allocative system for labor, the economy
could not have attained the vigorous growth it did.

Second, consider what is really meant by the *nenko*
("length-of-service") wage system. Wages that increase with
length of service or experience are not unique to Japanese
industries. They are seen widely in other industrial countries. In Western industrial countries wage rates increase
with promotion. In Japan wage rates that increase with age
or experience are also accompanied by increases in the
level of skill or status.

Figure 3.1 exhibits age-wage profiles for blue- and
white-collar workers with different educational levels for
both the United States and Japan. It shows that the Japanese age-wage profiles are quite similar to those of U.S.
workers except for the younger groups. It is interesting
that relative differentials between white- and blue-collar
workers are remarkably similar between the two countries,
suggesting that age-wage profiles are affected significantly

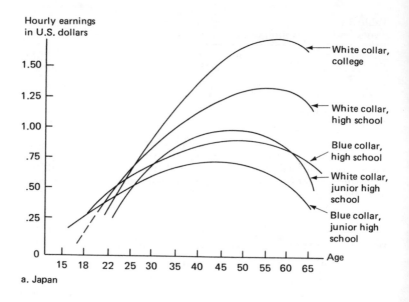

a. Japan

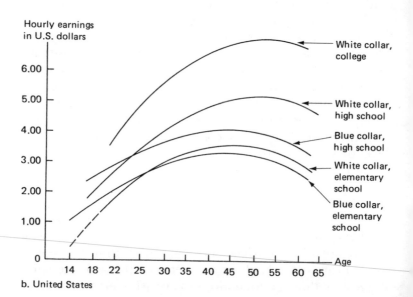

b. United States

by technological and organizational factors regardless of national differences.

The third element is enterprise unions. More than 90 percent of Japanese unions are organized on the basis of enterprises, and more than 80 percent of unionized workers are organized by such enterprise unions. This organizational form is probably unique to Japanese industrial relations.

However, the functions of these unions are not unique. Their main function is collective bargaining, just like their American counterparts. In fact the trade union law in Japan, which regulates union activities, was patterned after the labor relations law of the United States. If the function of enterprise unionism is to determine the working conditions of its members through collective bargaining, de facto equivalent practices are found quite widely in many other industrial countries. Collective bargaining at the firm level often occurs in the United States, and when it does it is functionally equivalent to what is done in Japan.

What is unique is a system of joint consultation by which management and worker representatives, usually union officials, exchange information on various matters relating to management policies, production plans, working conditions, fringe benefits, and the like.

This system is formally strictly distinguished from collective bargaining. It is the place for consultation and in-

Figure 3.1 (opposite)
Age-wage profiles in manufacturing industries of Japan and the United States. The figures are drawn using estimated parameters of wage equations fitted to the observed data. The equation is quadratic, with a squared variable for experience and an interaction term of education with experience. Source: Adapted from Haruo Shimada, *Earnings Structure and Human Investments* (Tokyo: Kogakusha, 1981), pp. 64–65. Basic data for Japan from Ministry of Labor, *Basic Survey of Wage Structures* (1967), and for the United States from Office of Economic Opportunity, *Survey of Economic Opportunity* (1967).

formation sharing and not for bargaining or making collective agreements.

According to a Ministry of Labor survey on labor-management communications conducted in 1977, more than 70 percent of the 5,000 private enterprises surveyed with 100 or more regular employees reported having a joint consultation system. Various surveys reveal that the system is more prevalent and more clearly defined the larger the size of the firm. In other words, the distinction between collective bargaining and joint consultation becomes less clear for smaller firms.

In many firms the consultation meeting is held fairly regularly, generally at least once a month. The issues discussed are mostly those directly related to working conditions, fringe benefits, and personnel matters, whereas issues reserved for managerial decisions such as management policies, financial matters, and investment in the plant are simply explained to labor representatives in most cases.

Areas of Missing Information

Conflicts

Unlike the popular image of harmony and consensus, Japanese society and industrial relations contain ample elements of frustration, confrontation, and conflict—perhaps exemplified by well-publicized violence and struggles that delayed the opening of Tokyo International Airport for more than a decade. Indeed, an examination of modern Japanese society will reveal ample evidence of social strife. Japanese society has been far from a harmonious or consensual society.

Even limiting our focus to the arena of industrial relations, we can point to many incidences of bitter labor struggles, at least up until the mid-1960s. One measure of the degree of industrial conflicts is the number of man-days lost during a year due to labor disputes. The average for the 1970s in Japan was 1.1 for every 10 man years. This is much lower than the 5.1 for the United States or the 5.8 for the United Kingdom for the same period—but much higher than the 0.5 recorded for West Germany.

In retrospect, however, the data give quite a different impression: 1.0 for 1965–1969, 1.8 for 1960–1964, 2.6 for 1955–1959, 4.5 for 1950–1954, and 4.6 for the late 1940s. In other words, during the first decade after the war, Japanese industrial relations were quite conflictive. The situation did not change markedly until the late 1950s.

Peaceful industrial relations are not as widespread as they are often depicted and even these peaceful and successful industries such as steel, shipbuilding, autos, and electronics, did not enjoy industrial peace until the mid-1960s. Industrial peace is maintained very carefully on a very delicate power balance even for these relatively successful industries.

Unsuccessful Cases
There are also innumerable cases of business failures side by side with success stories. Many of these unsuccessful cases are characterized by management's poor judgment and leadership, hostile labor-management relations, stagnant organization, poor human resource development, defective financing policies, poor policies for technological change, inappropriate management of production cost accounting and distribution.

Information on these failures is extremely limited even within Japan. This lack precludes a systematic examination of the critical elements and conditions that made some Japanese industries and firms successful.

Small Firms and Subcontractors
Large Japanese firms such as those in automobiles also use small firms as subcontractors. But information as to actual conditions in these small firms is extremely scarce. Marxist economists often claim that workers in these firms are vic-

tims of exploitation. We simply do not know. Nor do we have information on technological innovation, human capital development, competition, and other important aspects of management in these small firms.

Public Sector

Business corporations in private industries have been studied intensively, but much less attention has been paid to the public sector. Although the size of the public sector is relatively small in the Japanese economy, it nevertheless exerts important influences on the general model of Japanese industrial relations—both as the largest employer in the country and as the prime pattern setter for working conditions. If we had more information about this sector, it would probably show little difference from the public sectors in Western industrialized countries. Differences certainly exist, but they are only a matter of degree. Basic principles and structures of industrial relations and labor markets are largely similar.

As a result the highly successful segment of the economy that foreigners pay so much attention to in industrial relations is actually a relatively limited sector of the economy. Not all Japanese enjoy successful and trustful industrial relations simply because they were born Japanese.

Even after recognizing this heterogeneity and the complexity of actual industrial relations in Japan and their basic comparability with industrial relations systems of other countries, one may still wish to ask why and how such a successful achievement was possible in a relatively limited section of strategically important industries.

Crisis Consciousness in Japanese Industrial Growth

The Japanese economy survived drastic external shocks in the 1970s chiefly because of powerful fundamentals that were built during the 1960s. The basis for such a development had in turn been laid out during the crisis-ridden 1950s.

One of the serious defects associated with anthropological explanations of Japanese industrial success is the tendency to relate the recent remarkable industrial performance directly by a short circuit with ancient cultural inheritances without paying due attention to what had been done during critical periods preceding the rapid growth.

This tendency is particularly conspicuous in foreign observers, perhaps because of an unfortunate imbalance of available information. Although information available in foreign countries on Japan is relatively abundant for the late 1940s, when Japan was occupied and controlled by the Allied Forces, and the period after the mid-1960s, when the economy started to exhibit phenomenal growth, outside observers have little information about the 1950s, the period during which the critical bases were built for the subsequent growth.

After the termination of the shallow and short-lived Korean War boom, the Japanese economy was faced with a difficult impasse. Although the economy was prepared again to participate in world markets—after dampening the postwar hyperinflation, restoring the free market system, and overcoming the destruction of World War II—it still was far from being able to attain economic independence. Under such circumstances Japan had to seek drastic measures to attain both economic independence and improvements in the standard of living.

Reflecting a national crisis and a popular desire to catch up with advanced Western nations, the country chose the strategy of promoting exports through industrial rationalization.

In any country public consciousness of a national crisis helps mobilize human and physical resources toward some national goal, much more powerfully than is possible in more normal times. The Japanese experience in the 1950s may be viewed as one such example. Interestingly this kind of public consciousness has been relatively long-lived in Japan and often revived in response to various external shocks such as the recent oil shock.

Although a crisis mentality may not have been the most important factor in generating vigorous industrial growth, it certainly was helpful in reinforcing the effects of other factors. Noteworthy is the fact that the basic conditions necessary for the subsequent industrial growth were prepared during this period: technological know-how to improve quality of products, cooperative labor-management relations that are now predominant in export-oriented major industries, information-sharing systems within the internal labor market of corporate organizations, and an industrial structure with an abnormally developed sector of basic material input industries.

Emphasis on Quality Goods

Management believed that the most important and promising strategy for success was to improve the quality of products. Production of high-quality goods at low cost was thought to be the key to winning international competition, and corporations systematically mobilized their human and physical resources to achieve this goal. The target was pursued by the introduction of foreign technological and managerial know-how, on the one hand, and massive investments to attain rationalization, on the other.

Business corporations eagerly learned industrial engineering techniques from the United States and European countries. They sent their engineering and managerial staffs abroad to learn such techniques. To name just a few well-known examples of technological transfer, we may recall the assistance of ARMCO to Fuji Steel Co., General Electric to Toshiba, Austin to Nissan, and Philips to Matsushita.

Investments for the purpose of rationalization during the 1950s were also large. An outstanding example was the first five-year rationalization plan for the steel industry, which started in 1951. By the completion of this project, major steel corporations had established an integrated mass production system equipped with strip rolling mills. This achievement was succeeded by the second rationalization plan. By the late 1950s the waves of large-scale investments and technological innovation spilled over to key industries—electric power, shipbuilding, petroleum chemicals, autos, and electrical equipment. Such investments were important to using technological innovations.

Simply learning techniques from foreign countries does not help improve production, however. What is important is implementing such techniques and industrial know-how in production. The experience of Japanese automakers is interesting in illuminating this point. Japanese automakers developed a unique system of supplying parts and materials, incorporating both outside suppliers and intrafirm organizations for the purpose of minimizing inventories. The system operates under the principle of "just-in-time" (minimizing inventory), which is most symbolically exemplified by the case of the Toyota method of production.

The basic principle of minimizing inventory is, however, not a new production management technique. But Japanese automakers seriously attempted to construct a complex social and technical system organizing many tiers of subcontracted parts suppliers and various branches of plant organization following basic principles of production and cost management yet gearing them effectively to specific local conditions. In order to achieve such a goal, the corporation had to secure the maximum degree of understanding and cooperation from its employees and the people in the local community.

Efficient production can be attained only by full utilization of human and physical resources. For this reason full cooperation of workers and unions is crucial to achieving the goal. To secure their motivation and understanding, Japanese corporations took advantage of reshaped labor-management relations and information-sharing systems.

Fostering New Labor-Management Relations

Labor-management relations up to the mid-1950s were far from peaceful or harmonious. Quite the contrary, they were hostile and adversarial. Labor unions were dominated largely by leftist or communist leaders, and there were a number of strikes.

With high inflation and economic disorder in the years immediately following World War II, unions emerged spontaneously in most large and medium-sized enterprises. They often resorted to strikes or even workers' control of production in order to protect workers' security. The *Sanbetsu-Kaigi* (Congress of Industrial Unions), organized in 1946 by communist leaders, quickly gained ascendency in organizing disputes in various sectors of the economy.

Bitter labor disputes swamped almost every major industry until the mid-1950s. There was a fifty-six-day strike of Toshiba unions, a power industry strike in 1946, an attempt at a general strike (quickly banned by the order of the Supreme Commander of Allied Forces) led by public sector workers in 1947, a postal workers' strike, antidismissal disputes at Hitachi, a strike by National Railway workers in the late 1940s, a sixty-three-day strike of coal miners, a Nissan strike in 1953, steel workers' strikes in 1954, and more. An average of 4.6 man-days was lost for every 10 workers in the late 1940s and 4.5 man-days in the first half of the 1950s.

Since the mid-1950s, however, there has been a change in the labor movement. Although it is difficult to provide a complete explanation of the causes, certainly critical facets can be described. In many cases enterprise unions were split in the prolonged bitter struggles underway. Hostility and antagonism developed among various groups of workers. Facing hardships, leftist leaders grew more radical and extreme. Rank-and-file workers, on the contrary, grew increasingly skeptical about the reliability and usefulness of these dogmatic views. Reflecting such rank-and-file views, a second union often gained more popularity than the original one.

It was at this time that in some industries, such as steel, auto, and shipbuilding, conscious attempts were made to foster new management-labor relations by young and alert labor leaders. They admitted the necessity of planning ahead for future cooperation with management. In response, management helped them with their organizing activities.

Through bitter struggles and painful experiences this new group of labor leaders gradually acquired popularity among increasingly broader segments of key industries. Many recently influential union leaders in major export-oriented industries grew out of this movement.

One such example is the steel industry. In the fall of 1957 the steel industry federation of unions, led by leftist leaders, organized a ninety-eight-hour strike, which failed to win any concession from management. In 1959 the union federation organized a forty-seven-day strike selectively at Nippon Kokan and Fuji Co. and was again defeated. As a result the leftist leadership eventually had to give way to a new, more realistic leadership led by Yoshiji Miyata. In this process of struggle those who were critical of radical leftists gradually but steadily increased. This development was backed up in various forms by management, who wished to develop new and constructive labor-management relations.

National organizations were reorganized. Criticism by four industry federations of unions within *Sōhyō* against the strikes of coal miners and power industry workers in 1952 eventually resulted in the formation of *Zeonrō-Kaigi* (All Japanese Congress of Unions), a confederation of more moderate unions. The top leadership of *Sōhyō* also shifted through the 1954 and 1955 elections from Minoru Takano, who emphasized political unionism involving community actions, to Kaoru Ohta and Akira Iwai, who advocated economic unionism.

The new labor-management relations promoted by these movements, particularly at the levels of the firm and workplace now provided an arena for intensive and productive interactions between management and labor.

Development of Information-Sharing Systems

A number of new labor-management devices were developed and put into practice. Three notable examples are the joint consultation system, the role of first-line supervisor, and the well-known quality control (QC) circle movement.

The joint consultation system is an important vehicle for communication between management and labor on critical issues affecting the corporation and therefore the workers themselves. Unlike collective bargaining, joint consultation is used not for negotiation but for management and worker representatives to discuss a broad spectrum of issues, ranging from such large topics as investment and production plans to more specific issues like revisions of housing allowances. In some cases top management releases highly confidential information to union leaders at such meetings at a relatively early stage of the decision-making process in order to enlist the cooperation of the union. In other cases worker representatives provide alternative plans in order to make their standpoint clearer and to seek better understanding from management.

Introduction of the joint consultation system was first proposed by management after the war as a means to counter the workers' control of production advocated by radical labor leaders. It was not, however, until after the mid-1950s, when the new type of labor-management relations were constructed in major manufacturing industries, that the system started to prevail broadly. The campaign of the Japan Productivity Center, founded with U.S. help, was highly instrumental in promoting this trend.

Currently more than 70 percent of private enterprises with 100 or more employees have adopted the system as a standing organ. Many large firms have a well-developed and well-defined joint consultation system, which is clearly distinguished from collective bargaining; the distinction becomes less clear as the size of the firm gets smaller. Nevertheless, the joint consultations system is an important element in a complex system of information sharing.

The role of first-line supervisor is also important. First-line supervisors have dual roles in Japanese business organizations; they are the lowest-level manager and the highest-level worker—leaders of production teams.

The formalization of the first-line supervisor's role was also developed during the 1950s. Responding to the desire of management to restore systematic order at the workplace level, management attempted various training programs with the backing of the Japan Federation of Employers Associations in the 1950s. The need to establish some systematic order in the workshop was felt even more keenly as industrial rationalization proceeded. Responding to such a need, various attempts were made in many industries to enrich and strengthen the role of first-line supervisors. A well-known example of such developments is the introduction of the foreman system, learned from the United States, into steel corporations (Yawata Co., 1956 and Nippon Kokan Co., 1959).

Although the foreman system was patterned after the U.S. model, the Japanese foreman system has an important practical difference: Japanese foremen almost always are promoted from the ranks of production workers after accumulating long service and broad experience, and consequently they are very well informed about the business organization as a whole. Foremen often perform an integral role in transmitting information back and forth between management and labor and in sharing information among workers themselves in the workshop. By contrast, in the United States the role of foreman is limited partly because many of them acquire the position without necessarily accumulating as much experience as their Japanese counterparts and partly because their role as management is much more emphasized vis-à-vis their role as leader of the work group.

The quality control circle activities are designed to improve products. They can contribute to quality improvements by finding the best way of combining the abilities and characteristics of members of the work team. In the process of finding out different traits of workers by working and learning together, the activity also served the function of mutual communication and information.

The QC circle movement, which began in the early 1960s, has grown rapidly; there were 33,000 QC circles (400,000 partcipants) in 1970 and 115,000 (more than a million participants) in 1980. This growth reflects the rapid spillover of information-sharing systems in the workplace through informal group activities developed on the basis of structural reforms of work organizations promoted in the 1950s.

One of the outstanding features, and perhaps the most important feature, of Japanese business corporations is found in their highly internalized system of human capital development for production workers. The practice of long-term employment and internal promotion is not unique to Japanese corporations; it is found widely in large corporations in the United States and European countries. However, the uniqueness associated with the Japanese practice is the relative breadth of occupational experience while serving within the same company. A Japanese production worker typically is rotated among a relatively broader range of different job assignments within a company compared to his European or American counterparts. An important result of this practice is that Japanese workers tend to have greater opportunities to learn about relationships among different jobs. This aspect is constantly reinforced by in-company training and education.

A number of hypotheses have been proposed to explain why this type of employment practice is prevalent in large Japanese corporations. Some attribute it to the fact that many of Japan's leading corporations, which started out by importing foreign technologies in prewar and postwar days, had to develop skilled workers within their internal labor markets since no trained workers were available outside the firms. Others emphasize the role of postwar social reforms and union movement by which the status of blue-collar workers was elevated appreciably.

These employment practices, and the emphasis on internal training, have provided Japanese workers with a capacity to share information with management and to participate willingly in an effort to improve production.

Industrial Structure and Industrial Policies

A peculiar feature of the Japanese industrial structure that has contributed importantly to improving productivity is a highly developed sector of intermediate material input industries. Production of intermediate-input materials such as steel and petrochemical products can enjoy economies of scale. This means that the larger the capacity of production, the higher the productivity and thus the cheaper the price. Japan, which has to import most raw materials for industrial production, has sought to overcome this disadvantage by pursuing the benefits of economy of scale. As a consequence Japan has established an industrial structure with an abnormally large sector of intermediate-input industries, equipped with large-scale production facilities.

This structure provides price advantages not only to these intermediate-input industries themselves but also to industries that use the intermediate inputs. Steel is an example of such intermediate inputs; industries such as auto or shipbuilding can improve their productivity and the quality of their products by taking advantage of cheap high-quality steel sheets. In this regard the oligopolistic yet highly competitive nature of Japanese industrial organization was instrumental in keeping prices low through strenuous competition among producers.

The government also played an integral role by formulating industrial policies designed to guide the formation of this type of industrial structures and to maintain a reasonable degree of competition within industries.

The industrial policies of the Japanese government have attracted broad attention throughout the rest of the world, with a notorious connotation of "Japan, Inc." This image suggests that close ties exist between the government and businesses. Although it is true that the Japanese government exerted strong direct controls over industrial activities during postwar reconstruction, the mode of control shifted with the development of the economy toward utilizing the competitive function of markets. The most significant characteristic of Japanese economic and industrial policies may be found in the fact that the government collects, interprets, and disseminates relevant information to certain sectors of the economy, essentially to pave the way for the market to operate efficiently under given resource constraints. Had the Japanese industrial policies not operated to take advantage of market principles, it would not have been possible for Japan to attain such vigorous growth during the 1960s.

In the case of Japan a unique industrial structure and the mode of coordination necessitated by strenuous competition have contributed appreciably to increasing manufacturing productivity. Although this aspect is often overlooked in the discussion of corporate performance, it may have been the most important factor responsible for productivity improvement of Japanese firms. Notable is the fact that this factor developed during the 1950s.

Several background factors are often cited to explain the remarkable industrial growth of the postwar period: total physical destruction by the war provided Japanese industries an opportunity to reequip with newer and more productive facilities than their competitors; the social and political impact of the defeat in the war was helpful in introducing somewhat idealistic legal frameworks to maintain reasonable competition in labor and product markets and an abundant young and well-educated labor force; and lack of domestic resources made the Japanese look for cheap overseas raw materials and energy resources.

However, without active and positive efforts on the part of entrepreneurs, workers, and policymakers, these background factors may well have worked not as helpful factors but as hindrances. It is on the basis of this powerful industrial achievement that some segments of Japanese firms now enjoy peaceful, harmonious, and productive labor-management relations.

Conclusion

The style of Japanese management and industrial relations may appear to be strongly influenced by peculiarly Japanese humanistic characteristics and cultural inheritances. But in fact there exist many companies in Japan that practice typically Japanese-style management and industrial relations and yet perform only poorly. In other words, style and industrial success are two different matters.

Japan's industrial success has been attained by intentionally constructing with considerable costs and effort the basic conditions necessary for economic success. The structure and organization of production built within the Japanese economy during the preparatory 1950s and the rapid-growth 1960s is a monumental achievement in the industrial history of the world—economically, technologically, and from the viewpoint of social engineering. The success that attracts foreign attention is simply the result of the operation of such a remarkable system. It is neither luck nor miracle, nor is it historical inheritance.

If this is indeed the case, we may find two important policy implications. One is the transferability of such experiences. If industrial success has been achieved through intentional and rational efforts by the Japanese to overcome a perceived crisis rather than destined by humanistic and cultural traits, Japan's experience should contain elements that other countries will find useful. The sharing, however, is not in the form of superficial management styles as such but rather in the sense of how economically and technologically rational choices were realized in actual social and political processes of the society by intentional efforts.

The other relates to the future choices for Japan. To the extent that success was achieved under certain conditions in the past, it will not necessarily be guaranteed for the future. Indeed, in sharp contrast to relatively successful industries such as auto and electronics, basic material industries such as petrochemicals, aluminum, copper, paper, pulp, and various branches of chemical industries are suffering seriously from changes in their external conditions. And even the relatively successful industries, which have acquired a large share in the world market, will not be able to operate without taking into account their impact on affected countries.

Whether the industrial success of Japan can be maintained for the future will depend on whether the Japanese economy and society can adapt effectively to new and different external conditions in the future.

Lester Thurow
Reblending the American Economic Mixture

Shimada emphasizes the extent to which lifetime employment, the length-of-service reward system, and enterprise unionism were built in the 1950s and 1960s as opposed to being inherited from ancient tradition. If one examines the Japanese system of pay and employment carefully, it is not as different from Western practice as it may at first seem. There are some pay differentials, there is some mobility, and lifetime employment does not really cover an entire lifetime even for that portion of the labor force that has it.

Reblending is possible. We are not stuck with the present American system. At the same time a crisis is helpful in the reblending because it makes people more willing to accept changes that are economically painful in the short run but beneficial in the long run. In Japan the crisis was the defeat of World War II. In the United States we will have to build our current economic problems into the moral equivalent of defeat so that people will be willing to make the necessary sacrifices.

Large changes were made in American institutions and practices when the Soviet Union became the first nation to launch a satellite. The U.S. education system was completely overhauled, government budgets reallocated, and new effort went into our space program. Sputnik was in the end a minor, if spectacular, defeat that galvanized attention and made Americans willing to change familiar ways. One of the current challenges of American leadership is to turn a far more important, but less spectacular, economic defeat into the same willingness to change and experiment.

We Americans still pay lip-service to the Horatio Alger myth, but we have in fact built a strong and impermeable barrier between workers on the shop or office floor and management. The Japanese system is far more open both to information flows and to personal movement across the management line than is ours. Everyone in Japan also has some experience with being on the nonmanagement side. Company presidents are often ex-union leaders in Japan, an event so rare that for all practical purposes it never occurs in the United States.

Starting at the bottom and learning the company from the ground up was an old American tradition. But it is one that has almost completely faded with the use of educational credentials for establishing differential starting positions. This tradition must be brought back to life using quality control circles and other forms of participatory management. These practices improve team spirit and the flow of information. More important, they reduce the worker-versus-management class society that we have been building imperceptibly. They will let us tap ideas and talent that we have been missing.

4

The Firm and the Market in Japan

Hiroyuki Itami

Our purpose is to examine how organizational (command) and market principles are used to allocate resources within the Japanese economy. Using this framework, we then compare how these two principles interact in the United States and Japan to explain where Japan's firms and their market organization have potential advantages and potential risks.

The Allocation of Labor

In Japan it is very difficult to lay off workers. As a consequence the external labor market has less influence on the total number of employees in a Japanese firm than in an American firm. But within the firm internal labor markets are well developed. Workers are flexibly reassigned to different types of jobs during their careers in the same firm.

By forfeiting management's right to regulate labor requirements to needs, the Japanese firm has acquired in return the right to operate its internal labor market more flexibly. The major benefit to the firm is the freedom to move workers among the various job classifications in the internal labor market. With little outside labor mobility this serves to increase the stock of technical skills available to the firm.

In contrast, the U.S. firm retains the right to adjust labor requirements by hiring and firing in the outside labor market. The U.S. system performs economywide labor allocation by moving workers among firms. In compensation for this right, management has had to acquiesce in more inflexible arrangements that restrict the reallocation of the workers to different types of jobs within the firm. In effect this concession has prevented the fullest development of the firm's internal labor market.

In Japan mobility of labor among firms is not so extensive (the firm has less flexibility in hiring and firing), but the firm has more freedom in reallocating labor inside the firm. When the two are put together, the Japanese firm may enjoy more flexibility in adjusting the quality of its labor force.

In contrast, in America the firm benefits from greater mobility (quantitative flexibility) of labor among firms but is restricted in its internal reallocation (qualitative flexibility) of labor.

Interfirm Relationships

In the interrelationships among firms the relative weight of the command or organizational principles seems greater in Japan than in the United States. For instance, among a closely knit group of firms vertically organized under a dominant parent firm, the parent firm mitigates many conflicts of interest among cooperating subcontractors. The allocation process is best described as being done by the authority of the parent firm. The organizational character of the activities of the entire group—subcontractors and chief vendors affiliated with the parent firm—is highly developed. Sometimes there is also a strong sense of sharing in a commonality of purpose among Japanese firms in the same industry.

The Japanese government's administrative guidance is another case in point. It often is used to influence heavily firm or industry decisions.

United States policy in contrast seems to be to ensure the primacy of the market. One piece of evidence is the nation's enforcement of antitrust laws. Similarly in resource allocation within the firm, American firms seem to use transfer-pricing systems and divisional profit centers much more often than their Japanese counterparts.

At the same time government's formal regulation of business activities is more extensive in the United States than in Japan. The U.S. government's interference with market transactions often takes the form of putting direct legal restrictions on the firm's activities, whereas in Japan the government acts as a mediator of conflicting interests.

Allocation of Capital

A major characteristic of the allocation of funds among firms in Japan is the extent and depth of the bank's involvement in the process. The funds are gathered by the bank from investors and depositors and then allocated to borrowing firms. Since there exists a highly intimate continual relationship between the bank and the firm, the economywide allocation of funds to the Japanese firm is more of the nature of a quasi-organizational transaction rather than an arm's-length transaction in a pure capital market.

In comparison the relation between the capital market and the firm in the United States more closely resembles that of a pure market relation. Internal capital markets also seem more developed in the United States than in Japan. This is evident from the fact that the internal financing ratio of the U.S. firm is much greater than that of the Japanese. The more developed internal capital market is also illustrated by the great number of conglomerates in the United States. Conglomerates are almost nonexistent in Japan.

The importance placed by the U.S. firm on return on investment (ROI) in the allocation of internal funds is also a reminder that the allocation of internal funds is colored by pricelike mechanisms. In Japan the allocation of funds within the firm seems to be implemented much more in accordance with organizational principles.

Thus in the United States capital allocation within the firm and within the economy reflect the market principle more than they do in Japan. Both internally and externally organizational principles seem relatively more important in capital allocation in Japan than in the United States.

In many ways the allocation of capital and labor are mirror images of each other in the two countries. Internal capital financing is much greater in the United States than in Japan, whereas external labor mobility among firms is much greater in the United States than in Japan. This means that the relative weight of the firm as an arena for capital allocation is greater in the United States than in Japan, and the outside market's weight as an arena for capital allocation is greater in Japan than in the United States.

In applying market principles to the internal allocation of resources, the Japanese are ahead when it comes to the allocation of labor, whereas the U.S. firm is ahead when it comes to the allocation of investment funds. Although admittedly an oversimplified generalization, this seems to have important implications for the long-run ability of the firm to adapt to changes in the external environment.

The Ultimate Advantage

In an economy the ultimate driving force for growth and adaptation resides in the human resources that can embody an accumulation of technology. The human resource harbors and nurtures the potential for unlimited development, which money alone cannot buy. This is vital. To grow and to adapt, human resources must be managed so as to maximize the use and accumulation of knowledge.

The fact that the status of the personnel manager is very high in the Japanese managerial hierarchy seems to imply that the human resource occupies the central position in resource allocation within the Japanese firm. In contrast, in the United States the central concern for internal capital allocation appears to have been symbolized by the high status held by the financial officer in the American management hierarchy. This is also reflected in the much greater attention U.S. management pays to fluctuations in corporate stock prices as an index for appraising corporate performance, even though the equity market's importance as a means for corporate financing does not differ to any great extent between the United States and Japan.

The importance of finance in American management may hinder the better development and accumulation of human resources and technological knowledge.

Diversification Strategies

With labor the central element in Japanese internal resource allocation, and capital in the United States, an interesting task would be to discover how these differences are manifested in the firm's activities. These differences in fact may account for the differences in the diversification strategies of U.S. and Japanese firms.

The most important effect of the internal allocation of labor is that it serves to increase each employee's firm-specific skills and knowledge. Clearly in the Japanese firm periodic transfers of employees to various jobs within the firm increase their versatility, expanding their skills and experience. The beneficial effect of this job mobility is conspicuous among employees both in the shop and in the middle-management ranks.

In most Japanese firms plans for capital investment originate with the lowest-ranking suborganization in the firm and are then passed upward through the hierarchy until they reach the board of directors for final approval. This is the so-called bottom-up system.

Say the firm plans on introducing a new line of products, as part of its product diversification plan. A draft of the plan is prepared by the lowest suborganization. As it is channeled up through the firm, informal communications are exchanged among the different hierarchical levels to arrive at a consensus. At each level in the organization its contents are reviewed and approved or resubmitted after adjustments are made. In this process of successive adjustment there is nevertheless aggressive competition among divisions reflecting what in the United States would occur in the external market.

If a firm copes with the gradually shifting demand for new products with this type of organization and decision-making procedure, the resulting diversification strategy inevitably will be organically related to the main line of business. Even if there is a prospect for a new product with large potential demand, it will tend not to be considered unless it is in some way related to the firm's main line of business, for there is no one to advocate the case for completely new activities.

In establishing new businesses, accumulated technologies will be employed to the fullest extent, and existing interfirm relationships with cooperating subcontractors will be used. The bottom-up decision-making process also helps incorporate the past experiences of employees into the project plan and builds the basis for collaboration in its implementation among the subunits of the organization. Since labor is mobile internally, the new business will be organically related to the firm's existing business even if the new business involves largely different types of skills and jobs. As a result new businesses that may appear to be different from the firm's main business are often related to it in some way.

The key to successful Japanese diversification depends on discovering the linkage of the main business to any prospective new one and planning to employ fully the firm's accumulated capabilities. Empirical studies on diversifications indicate that related diversifications have produced better economic performance than unrelated ones.

In contrast, the likely American pattern of diversification is dominated by capital considerations. Capital unlike labor, however, does not embody or accumulate technological skill and knowledge. The funds are firm specific only in the sense that they are at its management's total disposal and are invested in accordance with its corporate strategy.

Given the characteristics of the American firm's internal markets for labor and capital, geographical expansion is one avenue for the firm's development. This avenue is attractive because it requires only geographical extension of accumulated capital resources. If labor is necessary at overseas localities, the firm can hire employees there. That the firm can take this course of labor recruitment more readily for its overseas expansion is partly due to the nature of its internal labor market. It does not have to provide jobs for old American workers if it shuts down an American production facility and opens a foreign one.

The American firm also tends to diversify into businesses unrelated to its main product lines, as typified by conglomerates. This type of diversification is in sharp contrast to multinationalization, which involves only geographical extension of a firm's existing resources. The conglomerate transforms its resources by adding wholly unrelated activities to its existing portfolio of activities.

But both conglomerates and the multinational corporations have a similar strategic logic in the sense that they are highly demand oriented and are not interested in human resources. Even if a firm's employees are highly specialized, its diversification strategy may not try to deploy these existing resources but rather may try to enter markets solely based on the prospects for future demand.

The now-famous product portfolio management model strategy is based mainly on prospects for future demand. The new field of diversification is selected by management as if it were creating an investment portfolio of stocks. The funds required for the selected diversification plan are supplied by the firm's management out of its internal capital funds, which it can dispense at its own discretion. Competent personnel to run the new businesses are recruited from the external market. In short, except for capital, the resources needed for implementing the diversification plan are procured from the outside. Hence the success of this kind of diversification depends to a large extent on the quality of the corporate strategy. If corporate sales rise and the firm's management resources and capabilities undergo qualitative transformation with the injection of new blood, further growth occurs. But if the original strategic forecast proves mistaken, there remains little margin for fine-tuning or integrating the activity with the firm's other businesses to cope with the problem.

In contrast, in a typical Japanese diversification the firm can better adapt to environmental changes because its strategy tends to be to enter new businesses related to the existing businesses. Human resources can be transferred between different activities.

The success of this Japanese type of corporate strategy is premised on several conditions. The first is that demand changes not be too abrupt and of the fine-tuning type. The second condition is that the economy grows at a certain speed so that the long-run growth in demand is assured. Unless these conditions are met, the firm's fine-tuning diversification strategy, which fits in-house competition in the internal labor market, will not be workable.

Sustained economic growth is important because it reduces the need for layoffs. The Japanese firm has abandoned the right to adjust its labor requirements by dismissing redundant employees but has achieved flexibility by transferring employees among various jobs. However, the labor-adjusting mechanism for absorbing redundant labor within the Japanese firm ceases to function if the firm is confronted too often with severe economic setbacks.

The Japanese and the U.S. Market Models

The Japanese market is penetrated by the organization principle in various forms such as the government's administrative guidance to firms, the self-regulatory activities of industry associations, and the cooperating subcontractors affiliated with a major parent firm. Here we shall not examine the problems created by this situation or evaluate its merits; instead, we focus on why the organization principle is so strong in Japan. We think it exists because it offers a solution to difficulties such as recessions.

Suppose a recession causes the size of the market to fall by 15 percent. In order to save the one or two firms confronted with bankruptcy, all firms in the industry will engage in industrywide consultation. They may decide to cut their respective outputs by 15 percent each, thereby each reducing income by 15 percent. The cartel creates a common cushion for absorbing the shock of the recession that no individual firm could create independently.

This Japanese way stands in contrast with the American one. In America a firm facing bankruptcy is regarded as a highly infected sore that needs to be surgically excised in order to ensure the survival of the rest. Bankruptcy would eliminate the least efficient firms, leaving the more efficient ones to survive.

But today no industrial societies can afford massive bankruptcies and the accompanying layoffs. Even if the individual firm could dismiss unwanted labor, the government, whose policy it is to uphold full employment, is charged with the responsibility of preventing unemployment. Consequently in the United States the protection of failing firms becomes a political imperative. Political protection of American domestic markets for steel and autos represent a prime example of the principle.

Of course the Japanese type of therapeutic solution that avoids surgical excision can weaken the viability of the industry and may lead to chronic illness in the end. In fact in the past the recurring cartels in some industries did have a weakening effect. However, the lessons of these past experiences have reduced the proclivity of firms to seek protection by means of the antirecession cartel. Furthermore Japan's Fair Trade Commission will no longer readily consent to the formation of such cartels. Hence current government policy allows antirecessionary cartels only under strict conditions and within a specific time limit.

Antirecession cartels can be characterized as backward looking in the sense that they are solutions for the crisis that have already occurred or are occurring. There are, however, more forward-looking measures used to inject organizational principles into the markets.

A case in point is a government-guided joint R & D program among otherwise competing firms. Because of large externalities associated with R & D, it is well known that there will be too little R & D if market principles are exclusively employed. On the other hand, if interfirm cooperative venture in R & D were allowed, there is risk that the cooperative will monopolistically not limit itself to R & D but will extend into the joint production and marketing of the product resulting from the new technology. Hence it is important that the market and the organization be combined in a way that eliminates these two dangers.

A successful example of such an arrangement is the case of the research cooperative for developing the VLSI (very large-scale integrated circuit) that had been formed by leading Japanese electronics firms. The cooperative was a joint venture of five major computer companies, a research institution, and an information company. It was established to develop the VLSI—the heart of future generations of computers. The cooperative's life was legally limited however and disbanded in April 1980 after it had accomplished its objective. The cooperative succeeded because it integrated the development capabilities of its member firms, competitors in the computer market, by providing a place for organized activities. But by limiting the cooperative's life, the resulting R & D did not degenerate into product collusion.

Conclusion

The operation of large Japanese firms is based on a competitive internal labor market that makes full use of a fixed labor force. The firm's growth strategy is adapted to this internal market because its diversification policy is organically linked to its main line of business.

There are two conditions necessary for these characteristics to be effective: (1) the reasonable and steady growth of the economy as a whole and (2) slowly changing patterns of demand. The economy must grow at a rate that does not drop substantially below, for example, 5 percent, the rate that many Japanese firms seem to anticipate. If the economy's anticipated growth slumps to 1 to 2 percent in the long run, as in Europe and the United States, then there is no assurance that the Japanese firm's organization and strategy can adapt smoothly to that state of the macro economy. The pattern of growth must also be such that demands will gradually change so that the firm can adapt by altering its strategy rather than by being forced to make drastic shifts in plans.

It is unlikely that Japanese firms can initiate radical innovations based on a strategy that foresees, for example, future life-styles and creates entirely new products to fulfill such needs. Many past examples seem to indicate that the U.S. firms are more competent with this type of behavior. The strength of the Japanese firm and the market is prem-

ised on steady economic growth and a fine-tuning adaptation to this growth.

This may also be a source of Japan's vulnerability.*

Lester Thurow
Reblending the American Economic Mixture

Every economy uses a mixture of market and organizational principles to allocate resources. The Japanese use
markets less to allocate labor across firms (with strict lifetime employment they would use it once for each worker,
whereas Americans would use it as often as they change
jobs), but they use markets more to allocate workers within
the firm's internal labor market. Since pay is tied not to
specific jobs but to seniority, there is more freedom to
move workers among jobs within the firm. Mobility is reduced in the external labor market to increase it in the
internal labor market.

In many ways this is a general Japanese pattern. At the
aggregate level there is more use of organizational principles—administrative guidance from the government,
heavy bank involvement in day-to-day business decisions—
but at a micro level there is less organization—fewer levels
of management, bottom-up management. Both have lessons for reblending the American economic mixture.

Although the market is good at making marginal
changes, it is often cumbersome when more drastic actions
are needed. Consider the issue of recession cartels where
the market for some products has permanently declined

*This is an edited and condensed version of a major part of "The
Firm and the Market in Japan—Mutual Penetration of Market
Principle and Organization Principle" by Ken-ichi Imai and Hiroyuki
Itami, Discussion Paper, Institute of Business Research, Hitotsuba-
shi University. Hiroyuki Itami presented this paper at the MIT
Symposium. The original paper will appear in full in an academic
journal in the near future.

and production must be cut back—let us say from five to three firms. The market ultimately will accomplish the desired result. Each of the five firms will be forced to lose money until the two financially weakest firms have been driven out of business. The major problem with this procedure is that often the three remaining firms have been so weakened by the necessary period of economic losses that they are unable to compete against the rest of the world; they cannot make the necessary investments to return to economic health. They survive but are deathly ill. The obvious solution is to work with the market to speed it up rather than trying to work against the market to save the two firms that cannot be saved.

In Japan government funds are used to lubricate the system in recession cartels so that production facilities will be withdrawn from production more quickly and to ensure that the economically strongest, not necessarily identical with the financially strongest, firms survive. The newest production facilities are also transferred promptly to the surviving firms.

Triage is a common practice in the medical field but not often enough used in economics. It is a tough medicine to apply but one that is occasionally necessary. One might argue, for example, that if farm incomes are not going to recover in the foreseeable future, it would be better for America to speed up the demise of International Harvester and reduce the losses now being suffered at John Deere and Caterpillar so that they can better compete with Komatsu in the future.

Although Americans universally preach that the market is always better than the organization, it is not a message that we can universally practice in a competitive world where we want American firms to be winners. The problem is to know when to take advantage of the advantages of both market and organizational principles.

5

The Japanese Financial System: Past, Present, and Future

Shoichi Royama

The Japanese financial system is in a process of rapid transition under the influence of growing international competition and the rapid progress of the economy itself. My aim is to follow transition of the Japanese financial system and to describe where the system seems headed.

Because the structure of financial markets and institutions in Japan was strongly influenced by government policy, it might be assumed that the process of transition has also been led by public policy. But the facts are not so simple. Complicated conflicts have occurred among those with vested interests in the old structure. The Japanese bureaucracy has basically been losing its leadership as the government becomes just one of the powers—rather than the power.

Postwar Japanese Financial Phenomena and Their Causes

Although there are many distinguishing features of the financial system of Japan after World War II, four facts are central.

The first is the dominance of the banks and indirect finance. Until the mid-1970s about 60 percent of total funds supplied by the financial markets were supplied through banks. Ten percent were supplied through non-bank financial intermediaries such as insurance companies, 20 percent were supplied through public financial institutions, and only 10 percent of total funds were raised in the stock or bond markets. In comparison about 40 percent of total funds have been supplied through stock and bond markets in the United States.

Second, the corporate sector, which had been the largest borrower of funds until the mid-1970s, relied heavily on bank borrowings. The high corporate borrowing rate in Japan would have been considered too risky in the United States. Even in Japan it is commonly called "overborrowing."

The third and fourth noteworthy characteristics of Japanese financing are found in the banking sector. Two groups of banks have shown remarkably different behavior in the short-term money market. One group, which consists of city banks and other big banks, has persistently borrowed in the call-money and the interbank discount market. The other group, consisting of various small- and medium-sized banks, has consistently lent in those markets. The money market among banks has become a permanent channel of funds from small and medium banks to big banks.

The Bank of Japan (BOJ) has given credit to city banks and other big banks exclusively. It has never given credit to other banks. Such credits have been the main route for increasing the supply of high-powered money.

Under this system the big banks have relied on borrowings from the central bank and interbank borrowings in the money market for most of their funds. In Japan this is known as an "overloan."

These characteristics are often regarded as unsound or undesirable by financial specialists in Japan. The choice of words reveals their judgments. An overloan, for instance, means that loans are extended in excess of what would be appropriate given prudent loan-to-deposit ratios. The overloan itself, however, is not a problem. It is merely a symptom of more basic issues.

To discover these issues, it is necessary to examine the factors that caused these four characteristics to emerge. The first cause is found in the high rate of economic growth, led by corporate investments and exports. The second is found in the rules and regulations issued by the Ministry of Finance (MOF) and the Bank of Japan.

The Artificial Low Interest Rate Policy

The system of financial regulations and controls has been called the artificial low interest rate policy. The Bank of Japan and the Ministry of Finance have basically created a system of segmented capital markets. Lending activities of each bank have been segmented by law. Specialization in some part of the lending business has been assured to each type of bank by law.

In addition interest rates have been controlled by the government. Most, but not all, interest rates are regulated directly by the government or determined by the bilateral bargaining of the participants under government tutelage. The workings of this system is key to understanding the Japanese financial system.

If all rates of interest and prices of financial assets were directly regulated by the government, conflicts of interest in the demand for or the supply of financial funds would have to be resolved by noneconomic factors. Politics would dominate the financial system. But in fact all rates have not been controlled.

In Japan, where banks play a dominant role, the deposit and the loan markets are the major funds markets. The deposit market has been opened to all banks. There are so many depositors in the economy that it is not possible to assign them to specific institutions, but deposit rates have been under the strict control of the government. Even the number and the location of bank branches (the most effective nonprice means in the long run) have been so well controlled by MOF that banks must compete for depositors in very restrictive ways, such as offering gifts.

In contrast, market segmentation is rather easy in the bank lending market. Ceilings were placed on some loan rates by the temporary interest rate adjustment law enacted in 1947. This maximum rate system was abolished and a standard rate system was introduced in 1959. Then in 1975 the cartel-like agreement among banks for setting the standard rate was abolished. The rate of interest on bank loans is now determined by negotiation between banks and their customer. The so-called prime rate, which is the loan rate on bills of especially high credit standard, is determined by the price leader among the banks. Usually the leader is the chairman bank of the Federation of Bankers' Association. It adjusts the prime rate to changes in the bank rate.

This does not mean, however, that bank loan rates in Japan are determined by competitive market forces. Rather Japanese loan rates are strongly dominated by person-to-person relations. Though Japanese banks have lost the formal backing of their interest rate cartel, there remain other factors supporting the rigidity of the loan rate. First, bank loan markets are far from perfectly competitive. Second, big banks are conscious of their ranking in the Japanese banking industry and do not rely entirely on demand-supply relationships in making loans. Third, a quasi-price mechanism works once basic interest rates on bank lendings have been established. The common custom of compensating balances has been used in Japan as a means to allocate real lending, rather than to affect real interest rates as is its more common use abroad.

One may argue that a quasi-price mechanism with compensating balances acts like a flexible interest rate system.

But it can also be argued that such a quasi-price system does not convey good information to third persons as to the effective loan rate. So there remains a question as to whether Japan's loan markets are adjusted by the market mechanism or by noneconomic credit rationing. There is as yet no agreement on this issue among the financial economists in Japan.

Given the system, it is natural that an interbank money market should develop to take the role of transfer of funds from temporary surplus to temporary deficit banks. In Japan the role of liquidity adjustment among banks has been taken by the call-money market. The interest rate on call-money has been rather free from the direct control of the government or the central bank. But as the transaction takes the form of transferring deposits at the BOJ or private banks, the participants have been so institutionally restricted that the market-determined call-money rate has had little influence on other regulated rates of interest.

Moreover, since the BOJ has kept its bank rate below the call-money rate as one of the main parts of its artificial low interest rate policy, it has been advantageous for every bank to borrow from the BOJ as much as possible. As a result the BOJ has obtained the power to ration its credit to private banks and, using this power, has effectively controlled the private banks' lending to the public. So-called "window guidance" would not have been so effective if it were only a moral persuasion.

Thus the artificial low interest rate policy has been characterized by the following: (1) Strict fixing of rates of interest where segmentation is by nature difficult; (2) rather weak interest control where new entry is difficult or where segmentation, backed up by law and custom, is easily maintained.

Why has such a system been maintained in postwar Japan? Is such a system possible today in the United States? The answer is clearly no. The most crucial reason lies in the fact that until recently Japan has never had open financial

markets where anyone can participate and conduct transactions without considering his direct counterparts.

This system is further complicated by government
bonds. The government only began issuing bonds in 1965,
but their price was so high that rates of return on the new
issues had never been attractive to investors. But banks and
other financial institutions had been urged to take them on
the condition that BOJ would repurchase them after a
year. This was designed as compensation for the low interest rates. The volume of issue until 1975 was not so massive,
and the BOJ could perform this compensation without
disrupting its control of the money supply.

Response to New Conditions

In the postwar period the Japanese financial system had a
unique structure. Networks of bilateral financial relations
covered the whole financial system, and financial laws
helped to hold the bilateral relations together. Regulation
of interest rates was maintained because those unfavored
by the regulation were compensated, directly or indirectly.
Through these networks, financial resources were allocated to growing sectors of the economy.

Some argue that Japan could have enjoyed an even better economic performance if it had adopted the flexible
price mechanism in financing. But Japan did not use the
price mechanism during its postwar economic recovery.
And once the path of recovery and growth was secured, it
could not find an opportunity to change the financial
structure.

The years 1973 and 1974 were important for the Japanese economy and its financial system. The first oil crisis
put an end to the era of fast economic growth. Consumer
price inflation, accelerated by the mismanagement of
money supply, shot up to 25 percent. Fiscal, monetary, and
other anti-inflationary measures were taken to curb the
economy. The years of long stagnation began.

With inflation and stagnation it was difficult for Japan to maintain its unique financial structure. First, strong discontent arose concerning the lack of equal opportunity in the management of financial resources. The oil crisis and the ensuing inflation broke the compensation mechanism for the regulated deposit rates. During the inflationary period in 1973 and 1974 the public mood changed to one that no longer favored fixed low deposit rates. Because of the regulations that continued to separate markets, the general public's access to markets other than deposits was so limited that many individuals could not hedge against inflation and the real value of their deposits was depreciating.

Second, social values changed as the potential for economic growth shrunk. A growth-oriented public policy could not continue to work smoothly in allocating financial resources.

Third, the massive issue of government bonds after 1975 produced dissatisfaction among the banks. Now it has become quite difficult to follow the ten-year-old custom of issuing low yielding government bonds—new issues were too large. Table 5.1 shows the annual new issues of government long-term bonds and the oustanding balances in the private sector from 1970 to 1979. As the table shows, outstanding balances of government bonds began to increase rapidly after 1975.

Fourth, the main instrument of BOJ's monetary control shifted away from lending to the purchase of bonds. The composition of assets held by the BOJ is shown in table 5.2.

The effectiveness of the BOJ's traditional monetary policy has decreased. The BOJ no longer has a free hand in using its traditional tools. Strong and varied political pressures make the job more difficult. As a result the BOJ introduces the market mechanism. It believes it can control the money supply more effectively and independently through open market operations.

Table 5.1
Government bonds after 1970 (billion yen)

Fiscal year	New issues	Outstanding (ratio to GNP)	Oustanding in the private sector
1970	355.7	2,811.1 (3.7)	520.8 (18.5)
1971	1,208.9	3,952.1 (4.8)	1,529.8 (38.7)
1972	1,967.4	5,818.6 (6.0)	3,215.1 (55.3)
1973	1,800.0	6,943.6 (5.9)	1,777.7 (25.6)
1974	2,200.1	8,403.6 (6.0)	1,328.9 (15.8)
1975	5,362.7	13,295.4 (8.7)	5,018.8 (37.8)
1976	7,148.0	20,023.1 (11.7)	10,933.4 (54.6)
1977	9,866.3	29,534.4 (15.5)	17,964.0 (60.8)
1978	10,792.1	39,612.0 (18.9)	26,436.8 (66.7)
1979	13,635.5	53,247.6 (23.7)	36,542.3 (68.6)
1980	14,657.1	68,910.3 (28.8)	46,098.2 (66.9)
1981	13,883.1	81,176.2 (32.6)	47,532.08 (58.6)

Sources: Nomura Research Institute, *Annual Survey of Bonds Markets;* Bank of Japan, *Flow of Funds Accounts.*
Note: Figures in parentheses are percentages.

Table 5.2
Asset composition of BOJ (10 billion yen)

End of fiscal year	Total assets	Loans and bills discounted	Bills bought and government bonds
1970	642.9 (16.0)	36.6%	37.0
1971	772.0 (20.1)	8.8	20.0
1972	904.2 (17.1)	23.4	19.2
1973	1,247.3 (37.9)	18.2	50.3
1974	1,502.4 (20.5)	11.2	62.7
1975	1,562.4 (4.0)	11.4	62.2
1976	1,702.3 (9.0)	11.5	63.8
1977	1,855.1 (9.0)	12.1	69.8
1978	2,089.2 (12.6)	13.8	67.8
1979	2,226.5 (6.6)	11.0	75.5
1980	2,410.5 (8.3)	9.7	79.0
1981	2,506.4 (4.0)	5.9	82.8

Source: Bank of Japan, *Economic Statistics Annual.*

At the same time there is growing internationalization in the financial world. Today Japanese firms have the potential to supply and demand funds in overseas markets. The problem is to match and adjust these supply and demand conflicts. And the Japanese style of bilateral bargaining with explicit or implicit governmental intervention automatically becomes less efficient.

Thus the Japanese financial system is confronted with drastic changes in its environment. To make a transition to a new situation, there should be a political decision to reform the structure. But that is not easy to do.

Development of Money Markets

The most remarkable financial changes are found in the recent development of a short-term money market. The call-money market has been working as an interbank money market, but until the late 1970s no other market had developed for short-term nonbank financing. The Gensaki-trade (bond trade with repurchase agreement) which used to be limited to short-term financing for security companies has emerged as a more general means of short-term financing to banks, nonbank financial institutions, and business corporations, as well as security companies. The bilateral Gensaki trade has developed into a Gensaki market.

The Gensaki market expanded remarkably after 1973 because it was the only market where nonbank investors could hedge against inflation. But the development of the Gensaki market created serious problems for banks, particularly to big banks, because good customers (mainly business corporations with short-term surplus money) shifted their portfolios from bank deposits to Gensaki purchases. Security companies gained customers from banks. Because of the competition banks began to offer a new short-term instrument to their customers.

In 1979 the MOF gave permission for banks to issue negotiable certificates of deposit (CD) at rates where inter-

Table 5.3
Development of money market in terms of outstanding balances
(trillion yen)

End of calendar year	Call money	Bills bought and sold	Bonds with repurchase agreement	Certificates of deposit
1974	2.2	5.2	1.7	
1975	2.3	4.4	1.8	
1976	2.6	5.1	2.1	
1977	2.6	6.1	3.1	
1978	2.3	6.6	4.2	
1979	3.5	6.3	4.0	1.8
1980	4.1	6.1	4.5	2.3
1981	4.7	4.0	4.5	3.3

Source: Bank of Japan, *Monthly Review* (October 1980).

est could be determined by negotiations between the bank issuer and its customers. The MOF welcomed the new instrument because it helped banks accept new flotations of government bonds. In 1981 CDs gathered 4.6 percent of the total domestic deposits issued by banks.

Because of the development of new money market instruments, the existing interbank market has become less regulated. Instruments with different terms were introduced to interbank money markets. Quotations of interbank rates, which had been maintained by consensus between the largest demanders (city banks) and suppliers (financial institutions for agriculture, forestry, and fishery) under the implicit guidance of BOJ, were completely abolished in 1979. As a result the Japanese financial world began to have an open and well-organized money market system. The present scale of money markets is shown in table 5.3.

Expansion of Bond Markets
Massive flotations of national government bonds after 1975 required changes in traditional methods of financing. Medium-term (two- to five-year) bonds were being sold, some priced by auction.

A secondary market has also developed. Since the holders of bonds (especially banks) cannot liquidate them by selling them to the BOJ, a secondary market, with prices being freely set, was needed.

Until the mid-1970s banks were prohibited from selling their government bonds to the public, and the price of bonds was administered by MOF. As the outstanding government bonds became concentrated in the banks, however, the government eased the regulations concerning banks' bond holdings. In 1977 banks and other financial institutions were allowed to sell their government bonds if more than one year had passed since the bonds were floated. Now although MOF places some restriction on bank sales, deregulation has developed to a great degree. And these government bonds are forming the core of the secondary bond market in Japan.

The BOJ has also begun to invite tenders for its operations. The development has had a great influence on the floating price of bonds. Yield flexibility on government bonds is increased.

Thus a Japanese bond market has developed remarkably. The issuing market has expanded sevenfold in the past decade, reaching about 28 trillion yen in new issues during FY 1981. Transactions in the secondary market have become much more brisk. The annual volume of transactions exceeded 200 trillion yen in FY 1978 and 300 trillion yen in FY 1981.

The Japanese financial system seems to be moving toward a system dominated by an open money-bond market. The main feature of the changes is shown in table 5.4. The direct flow of funds from savings to investments is increasing, and indirect finance is losing its past dominant role. Bonds are assuming an increasingly important role as financial instruments in Japan.

Table 5.4
Changes in characteristics of the Japanese financial system (percent)

Calendar year	Indirect finance ratio	Outstanding securities to loan ratio	Proportion of bonds in securities
1964	82.0	24.7	33.1
1965	91.1	24.2	36.2
1966	94.5	24.9	44.0
1967	92.4	25.0	48.6
1968	91.1	24.8	50.8
1969	91.3	23.8	52.2
1970	88.3	22.7	52.8
1971	87.4	21.5	56.0
1972	95.1	21.1	58.7
1973	93.8	20.1	63.2
1974	90.4	20.4	65.5
1975	94.7	21.7	67.3
1976	92.1	23.1	71.9
1977	90.6	25.1	73.4
1978	88.5	27.8	72.8
1979	88.2	29.1	75.6
1980	88.7	29.6	77.1

Source: Bank of Japan, Flow of Funds Accounts.

Future of the Japanese Financial System

These recent responses of Japan's financial system to new conditions are quite natural. Social value judgments are now so diverse that past policy guidance becomes rather ineffective with regard to capital allocation. Impersonal adjustments by market mechanism are much more highly appreciated.

The BOJ has also come to believe that it could control the money supply better under a flexible price mechanism.

In the near future the Japanese financial system will be much more market oriented. Free competition in the market will determine the allocation of financial resources. Such a future prospect is predicted by almost all financial specialists. Difference in opinions exists only with regard to how Japan should make the transition toward a full market system. This difference in strategy, however, makes the path of change complicated.

Every financial institution in Japan has vested interests in the past structure. As a private organization, each wishes to keep the advantages and minimize the disadvantages. When the system has to be changed, some changes in the system are favored by some groups and not by others. In such a situation it is quite natural that the changes that actually occurred are the least disruptive. The most contentious issues, crucial as they are, are likely to be untouched without any effective resolution.

Further Development of Money Markets

Although the money market has become more open, the Gensaki and CDs are not the best open market instruments. Treasury bills (TB) should be the core of the market. Japan has treasury bills, but they are issued with such a low yield as to discourage buyers. Almost all are accepted by the BOJ. For fear of increasing government interest burdens, the MOF does not want to liberalize TBs, an attitude that will be put to the test within a couple of years.

The BOJ is challenging the MOF by selling its TBs at market prices. The first sales were made in May 1981. Nevertheless, the MOF is unhappy with this BOJ policy.

Redemptions of outstanding medium- and long-term government bonds started in FY 1980 with no serious difficulties, but the volume of maturing bonds will increase dramatically from year to year with a likely growth in government bonds of short maturities. This will lead to a secondary market for government bonds on much the same foundations as those for treasury bills. And it may lead to a severe conflict between the MOF and the BOJ over interest rates.

Revision of the Bank Law

Consideration is also underway to revising the bank law, which was first enacted in 1927. In 1975 the MOF asked the

Council on Financial System Research to make recommendations and the final report was submitted in 1979. The report, however, made no positive proposals for reform other than the introduction of CDs. It advocated deregulation, particularly lowering the institutional barriers of entry found in the present financial system, but did little about concrete issues.

If we consider the present situation little can be expected from the Council on Financial System Research. It can only deal with the private financial intermediaries. In the past when banks held the principal role in financing, the Council and the Banking Bureaus of the MOF were able to administer the policies of the financial system. But they no longer can.

Conflicts arise. A typical case concerns the Article 65 problem. Article 65 of the Security Exchange Law enacted in 1948 prohibits banks, trust companies, and other financial institutions from underwriting securities and from conducting securities businesses—with the exception of transactions of government bonds, local public bonds, and government-guaranteed debentures. Patterned after American law, this article was designed to separate the securities businesses from the banking business.

Because public bond markets were underdeveloped, banks rarely conducted market activities in public bonds. As previously described, the situation has changed. Securities transactions, including public bonds, have become promising business activities. Banks believe that they can use these markets to lessen their quasi-compulsory burden of government bonds holdings and that new flotation will be easier if they can sell government bonds.

Seizing the opportunity to revise the fifty-year old bank law, the banks have also tried to establish the legitimacy of their security transaction businesses. Bank bond sales will surely lead to the result that banks will become dealers as well as brokers on the bond market. Security companies, chartered brokers, dealers, and underwriters not surprisingly oppose such changes.

After the report by the Council on the Financial System Research in the summer of 1979, the Banking Bureau of MOF started to revise the bank law. The job was difficult, but finally in May 1981 the new bank law passed the Diet and became effective in April 1982. Under the new law a bank cannot extend loans of more than 20 percent of its capital and surplus funds to a single borrower. Disclosure of bank activities and financial situations are also recommended. Although the law contains many new articles, almost all of them are only ratifications of past administrative decisions. In many ways the new bank law can be regarded as the natural extension of the old legal and administrative system.

The Japanese financial system cannot evolve smoothly without national consensus as to the right long-term global strategy. Any piecemeal attempt to reform the system will be ineffective because of conflicts among vested interests. The development of money and bond market policies only ratified natural tendencies. Future policies of the financial system will not be able to maintain this passive attitude.

The new Foreign Exchange Law in 1980 makes available to both residents and nonresidents profitable investment opportunities in domestic and overseas markets. New financial instruments, particularly for large investors, will appear within a few years. In this way liberalization of financial markets leads to further liberalization. However, unless the past regulations and controls can adjust themselves to the new situation with a definite program for the future, those liberalizations may not be favorable to the economy as a whole.

The money and bond markets are at present only for financial institutions and business corporations handling large amounts of money. They are not easily accessible to small investors. Medium-term government bonds investment funds were introduced in 1980 by investment trust companies and supported by securities companies for small investors. But the MOF set an upper limit on the rate of return on the funds so that they did not have a favorable effect on small investors. Rather it highlighted the problem of inequitable investment opportunities.

Expansion of Postal Savings

The most troublesome new problem concerns the expansion of postal savings. The postal savings system has a long history; for more than one hundred years it has been an important source of funds for the Japanese government. The postal savings system was established in 1875 to provide savings opportunities for individuals anywhere in the country. Today 22,000 post offices located throughout Japan do postal savings business. Postal savings account for 20 percent of total individual savings. It offers several types of saving instruments. The most popular is the savings certificate which provides high liquidity and compound rates of interest. With present interest rates, savings certificates will surely yield higher interest rates than time and savings deposits at private banks if they are not liquidated within less than two and a half years. In addition postal savings of all kinds get preferable tax treatment, though a maximum limit is set on an individual postal savings holding.

After the first oil shock and the ensuing inflation, the Japanese people became sensitive to the rate of interest in their assets management. Postal savings, particularly savings certificates, turned out to be the most attractive savings commodity available to individual investors.

Encouraged by the increase in postal savings, the system has been trying to offer various financial services to customers such as personal loan programs. The aggressive management of the system, as well as the remarkable expansion of its savings, however, came into collision with private financial institutions. The city banks took a leading role in the movement against the postal savings system.

They claimed that government should eliminate the preferable treatment for postal savings and that rates of interest on postal savings should be regulated by the BOJ under the Temporary Interest Rate Adjustment Act in the same way as their deposit rates.

This conflict has not yet been resolved. The prime minister organized a committee to study the problem, but the report, submitted in autumn 1981, was too favorable to private financial institutions to persuade the Ministry of Postal Services to change its practices. The MOF is on the horns of a dilemma. On the one hand, because postal savings are the largest source of funds for its financial investment and loan program, it is quite favorably disposed to increases in postal savings. On the other hand, it should support the private financial institutions as their administrator. The issue is not easily settled within the present institutional structure.

The case would have been quite different if private financial institutions could have offered new financial commodities and services attractive to past customers. If they had, the shift of deposits from private banks to the postal savings system would have stopped. Indeed, some private banks tried to issue a new savings instrument for individuals at the time of the first oil crisis. The MOF and others, however, took a firm stand against the new instrument, and it took eight years for private institutions to reach a consensus.

In June 1981 the MOF permitted private banks to offer a new type of savings deposit like savings certificates. Since then private financial institutions other than banks have begun to compete with each other. But the competition is under the control of the MOF.

Changes in Japan's financial structure mean changes in government-bank-industry relations. The MOF is losing its directive power over bank management. Banks, particularly big banks, are being forced to adapt to the new system. In the past financing business corporations meant borrowing from banks. Now it means a greater variety of things. For those with a surplus of funds, financial investment is becoming an important business. Toyota for instance earned more than 50 percent of its annual income by successful portfolio management in 1981.

Conclusion

Only a global long-term vision of the future will enable the Japanese financial system to avoid the problems that confront it. The actual transition will be slow but incremental and should have nationwide consensus.

At present all groups (including foreign banks) participating in the Japanese financial system need to make clear their future objectives, and the government needs to set up a new organization to coordinate programs to meet these objectives. This organization should be under the direct administration of the cabinet. The present system of public administration cannot resolve any crucial structural reform. There are too many different bureaucracies with vested interests. The transition process of Japan's financial system will be distorted by conflicts among such vested interests.

The Japanese government should restore its position as coordinator. Those concerned with financing should declare some overall vision of the Japanese financial system. Otherwise, the transition toward a flexible-price financial system may fail.

Lester Thurow
Reblending the American Economic Mixture

Royama describes the Japanese financial system as moving from a system of credit allocation in which administrative guidance played a major role to one where the market plays a much larger role. What worked in the past is no longer possible in the future given a change in conditions. Although the Japanese can be described as evolving toward our system, this history should not be read as one that confirms the validity of the American financial system.

American conditions have also changed, and we have to determine whether what worked in the past will work in the future. What gaps need to be filled? A comparison of the American financial system with the Japanese system or with the system in any other industrial country will reveal a major difference. The rest of the world has investment banks, usually public and private; the United States has no investment banks. We have some Wall Street brokerage firms that call themselves investment banks, but they are not that. They are brokers who help match investors with savers; they have no substantial funds of their own to invest. Investment banks were made illegal in the 1930s because the public blamed the House of Morgan for the Great Depression. Whatever the truth to these charges (and there is very little), the American economy now needs investment banking.

Investment banks are a source of major amounts of long-term investment funds. They are not competitive with venture capitalists but complementary to them, raising funds necessary to catch a successful start-up through the period of rapid growth and investment necessary to become a major industrial firm. They also provide funds to get new operations going in areas where huge amounts of capital are necessary. Venture capital can finance a $50 million to $100 million electronic start-up, but it cannot finance a $2 billion start-up of a new state-of-the-art steel mill. Yet America wants to ensure that its successful new firms become successful big firms and that it is not systematically kept out of capital-intensive industries because its capital markets cannot provide the necessary finance in these areas.

Traditionally America's new start-ups in capital-intensive areas would be done by old-line firms: the existing steel companies would build the new steel mills. But this is no longer possible. The old steel companies, because they now have foreign competitors, may not have the funds to make such investments. And if the old steel companies have fallen behind technologically, there is no reason to believe that they have the human resources to bring new ideas into the marketplace. Investment banks can help solve these problems by either funding new companies or with their leverage and management altering the management of the old-line companies to make them effective vehicles of economic progress.

Although the American financial system is evolving because of our laws, it is not evolving toward investment banking. Rather it is evolving toward financial supermarkets that are almost entirely focused on consumers. Systems evolve, but they evolve within the channels set by society. Sometimes these channels need to be altered. This would seem to be one of those times.

Consider the Japanese long-term credit bank (a bank that if it were the same size relative to the American economy would have almost $300 billion worth of long-term equity lending) or any other investment bank around the world. Why do other countries need these institutions? Why is it that America can get along without them? Perhaps it cannot.

6

Product Diversification

Ichiro Hattori

Today corporations in every country are heavily involved in developing and implementing product diversification programs. Japan is no exception. A Japanese corporate diversification program, however, must be viewed in the context of the Japanese management environment—company-based unions, lifetime employment, seniority wages and promotions, and the employee's strong awareness of belonging to a corporate community. In order to demonstrate how this distinct management environment affects a corporation's diversification program, I will use Daini Seikosha Co., Ltd. (the company changed their name to Seiko Instruments & Electronics, Ltd., in 1983), one of the Seiko Group of companies, as an example.

The Seiko Group

Seiko-brand timepieces are manufactured by three companies—Daini Seikosha Co., Ltd., Suwa Seikosha Co., Ltd., and Seikosha Co., Ltd.—and sold throughout the world by K. Hattori & Co., Ltd. (The company changed their name to Hattori Seiko Co., Ltd., in 1983.) These three companies comprise the Seiko Group but they are not subordinate to one another. They are independent of one another although they share a common group of stockholders.

The fourth company, K. Hattori & Co., Ltd., has exclusive responsibility for the sales of watches and clocks, but products other than timepieces are supplied to the market by the marketing organizations of the three manufacturing entities of the Seiko Group.

Although the Seiko Group exchanges information and opinions regarding product diversification strategy, each company establishes its own autonomous program. In contrast, in the timepiece business the three manufacturing companies of the Seiko Group hammer out a comprehensive strategy while maintaining close liaison with K. Hattori & Co., Ltd. The Seiko Group is currently seeking a new path toward more diversified business activities.

History

The history of Seiko from the inauguration of K. Hattori & Co., Ltd., in 1881 up to the 1960s might well be described also as the history of timepieces. The great success of the Japanese watch industry has been due to two major factors: (1) the conversion of an old watch industry strongly colored by an artisan spirit into a modern industry, with mass-production techniques with high quality control systems, and (2) continuous research and development which gave birth to automatic mechanical watches and then to electronic watches.

From a marketing standpoint it cannot be overlooked that Seiko placed first in the International Chronometer Contest held in the 1960s and that Seiko brands were adopted as official timers for the 1964 Tokyo Olympic Games. These events attested to Seiko's technological power and attracted worldwide attention, and Seiko brands rapidly developed a reputation for excellence.

Up until the 1960s Seiko invested profits in product improvement. In the 1950s which was a period of postwar rehabilitation, our major objectives were to construct factories and establish precision machining techniques. During the 1960s we wrestled vigorously with the task of improving productivity and quality with mass-production techniques. In both productivity and quality we wanted to catch up with and surpass Switzerland.

Beginnings of Seiko's Diversification Strategy
But it is unrealistic to expect the watch industry to sustain its high growth for many more years to come. Therefore we decided to diversify into different technologies. The 1964 Tokyo Olympic Games marked the starting point for that diversification.

In particular, we had developed various special race-timer systems and record-indicator display systems for the Olympics. These technological developments bore fruit later in the form of digital printers, personal computers, and other products. The development and sales of digital printers by the Suwa Seikosha EPSON Group has provided an outstanding market success story. Today EPSON brands have captured 30 percent of the world market for terminal printers used with small computers and 70 percent for miniature printers used with cash registers, pocket calculators, and the like.

The manufacture and marketing of quartz electronic watches (both analog and digital) paved the way for diversification into electronic components, such as liquid crystal indicator panels, ICs, batteries, and quartz crystal oscillators. The development of the Seiko quartz electronic watch has enabled the Seiko Group to change from a watchmaker into a manufacturer of miniature-sized personal electronic appliances and instruments.

Diversified products manufactured by Daini Seikosha Co., Ltd., can be classified roughly into two categories: products evolving out of watchmaking and products introduced to enable the company to use techniques not now utilized in watchmaking. In the past the Seiko Group had to wrestle with precision machining techniques for processing mechanical parts needed in watches. Out of these in-house techniques evolved products such as precision machine tools, automatic assembly systems, and robots.

In new fields we now produce scientific gauges, audio equipment, and graphic display systems. These products are grounded in our precision machinery processing techniques. Analysis and measurement techniques utilizing electron beams, X-rays, and optical spectroscopy have developed out of our in-house techniques used to produce scientific instruments. Quartz techniques, vital to the production of timepieces, have lead to the production of quartz metronomes and quartz tuners.

Automatic drafting machines are indispensable to the development and production of precision instruments and parts. When graphic processing systems became automated as a result of progress in computer technology, we introduced automatic drafting machines. Later we developed with our own techniques a digitizer (an input apparatus) together with a plotter (an output apparatus) to produce an automatic graphic processing system. This system is actively utilized in computer-aided design (CAD) and has been widely adopted by Japanese semiconductor makers.

Management Strategy and Business Diversification

The 1970s was an important period for the Daini Seikosha group of companies. Since quartz wristwatches were being manufactured and marketed, the Daini Seikosha group had to reform its corporate structure to enable a change in production techniques from mechanical to electronic watches.

The change from mechanical to quartz watches involves a switch from precision machining techniques to electronic technology. Hence we had to reassign and reorient many employees while investing in new facilities for the production of liquid crystal panels, quartz crystal oscillators, batteries, semiconductors, and other electronic parts.

Since quartz electronic watches have fewer parts than mechanical watches, fewer people were needed in their production. As a result we had to ask employees to retire to ensure the necessary cost reductions. Meanwhile the oil crisis sparked a dramatic upswing in raw material and energy costs.

The corporate reform plans formulated by the Seiko Group companies to surmount these difficulties were launched in 1975, and it took about three years for the plans to attain tangible results.

As a result of these plans, Daini Seikosha Co., Ltd. succeeded in changing production techniques, renewing production facilities, and reducing its work force by about 1,000 employees (17 percent). The personnel retrenchment was successfully carried out by not hiring new workers for three years (except for technical staff needed because of new technologies) and by discharging older employees who had passed the retirement age.

Multidivisional Business Operations in the 1970s
Prior to reform new products other than wristwatches were launched in multidivisional business operations. These were carried out not so much on the basis of concrete goals set by top management but with the natural ability and interest of individual engineers and technical specialists leading the way. Multidivisional business operations actually took two forms: some products were developed freely from production techniques owned by the company, while other products were developed utilizing techniques that the company had not previously possessed. These multidivisional developments have allowed us to expand our operations to a wide range of precision electronic instruments.

The sales record shows that the Computer Graphic Division and Scientific Instruments Division did not really get underway until approximately five years ago. If we include the period of development research, this means that eight to ten years were required to secure the proper balance of development, production, and marketing.

The long time lag occurred because it was necessary to get a consensus of all the groups involved in multidivisional business operations. We always had some employees in the company who were strongly interested in the new area and helped promote it. Without these interested employees, it would have been much more difficult to initiate the new projects, and we would have had to hire new employees—in many ways an unsatisfactory solution.

Projects made smooth progress while still in the design stages, but it took time to establish production techniques. Market information could only be obtained by actually selling new products. And it was difficult to market single products no matter how excellent in quality unless the products could be supplied in variety. Daini Seikosha's sales appear in table 6.1.

The New Daini Seikosha Project
Daini Seikosha's management plan for the 1980s—called the New Daini (ND) Project—is to redesign its operations to cope with changes in the external environment.

The worldwide output of timepieces was 100 million pieces in 1960, 220 million pieces in 1975, 320 million pieces in 1980, and will be an estimated 500 million pieces in 1990. Japan's share in the world market was 88 million pieces in 1980, or about 27.5 percent. Seiko's share is about 14 percent and the Daini Seikosha group's share about half of that.

In terms of value Japan's market share is currently about $20 billion with an average retail price per piece of $62. But the distribution costs of watches is very high. In the export market the factory shipment price accounts for only about 20 percent of the retail price and therefore the market value at the factory level is about $4 billion.

Table 6.1
Daini Seikosha sales (million yen)

Year	Machine-tool parts		Computer graphics systems	Scientific instruments
	External sales	Total sales (including intracompany sales)		
1964	(136)	902		
1965	(260)	1,007		
1966	(349)	912		
1967	(553)	1,368		
1968	(556)	1,917		
1969	(528)	2,471		
1970	(934)	3,071		
1971	(761)	2,637	133	
1972	(780)	2,429	424	
1973	(1,209)	2,768	648	123
1974	(1,293)	3,620	542	589
1975	(858)	2,693	801	1,123
1976	(1,712)	2,356	1,164	1,045
1977	(1,710)	3,147	1,487	1,786
1978	(2,217)	3,330	2,246	2,561
1979	(2,701)	3,948	2,611	3,160
1980	(4,811)	6,490	3,416	4,507
1981	(7,375)	8,883	5,738	5,484

It is extremely difficult to predict the average retail price trend over the next ten years. More competition, expansion of the low-price market, and inflation will lead according to our estimates to a factory value of about $5.2 billion in 1990, or an expansion of only 30 percent in the next ten years.

We project the Seiko market share to be no more than 30 percent at the most. Thus the highest revenue we can expect of watches is about $2.4 billion.

But to produce these watches, how much revenue will be needed? We call such revenues the "survival line." If the company keeps operating at a value-added rate of 40 percent and labor's relative share is 63 percent with 20 percent more personnel, we must realize revenues amounting to 310 billion yen if wages rise at 7.5 percent per year. If the value-added rate drops to 30 percent and the company has 10 percent more employees, it must realize revenues amounting to 330 billion, assuming wages rise at 6 percent. Adding a risk premium because of price fluctuations, the survival line goes up to 370 billion yen. Unforeseen risks add another margin of some 30 billion yen to our survival line. The net result is that we have set 400 billion yen as our target revenue.

The target revenues break down into 200 billion yen in watch sales and 200 billion yen in diversified product sales. The basic concept of the ND Project is that the Seiko Group companies should restructure their activities so that they can move into other areas, though with watch or clock production remaining one of the core business activities.

The Japanese Management Climate and Multidivisional Business Operations

The most salient feature of Japanese business management lies in the social orientation of the corporation. The legal definition of a business corporation is the same in both Western countries and Japan (it is a business designed to realize profits to its owners), but at the same time an enterprise is an organization that assures its employees of their jobs and incomes.

In the United States management focuses on the realization of maximum profits. By contrast, in Japan a corporation is responsible for the creation and maintenance of employment. Most Japanese managers think that increasing profitability and providing benefits to employees are equally important.

The climate that has given birth to such business concepts is a product of company-based unions, lifetime employment, seniority-based wages and promotions, and the employees' strong awareness of belonging to a corporate community. Intracompany communications are essential to the formation of corporate consensus, and participation by subordinate organizations in the process of important decision making is given considerable weight. These elements of Japanese business management are often misunderstood abroad.

Company-Based Unions

Labor unions are organized by individual enterprises or by corporate groups, not by job type or industry. Individual labor unions belong to senior organizations, but senior organizations do not exercise strong control. Corporate working conditions are decided under an agreement concluded between the representatives of management and the labor union of the corporation. Because of this structure labor-management relations are not disturbed by external factors and can be maintained by internal efforts.

The company-based union system has merits, such as facilitating the transfer or rotation of employees, but at the same time the system generates the atmosphere of a closed society.

Lifetime Employment

We Japanese argue as to whether lifetime employment is a traditional virtue or a custom created during the era of economic high growth since World War II. I believe the latter are right. However, lifetime employment is not really that. Most corporations set a retirement age. Management, for its part, wants to place as many retiring employees as possible in outside jobs, but there are limits to such efforts. It is generally accepted that the retirement age of company executive officers averages seventy and that of other employees sixty.

Lifetime employment means stable employment—a management policy of maintaining employment security for employees until they reach retirement age—notwithstanding changes in business conditions. This policy of stable employment is strictly adhered to in large businesses.

When we compare Japan after the oil crisis in the 1970s, we find that the rate of unemployment was lower in Japan than abroad but that Japan suffered greater losses of corporate profits. This demonstrates that Japanese enterprises attach greater weight to job security than do their counterparts in the United States and Western Europe.

When layoffs do occur, many Japanese corporations ensure that laid-off employees get more than 80 percent of their normal wages, and some corporations pay such employees 100 percent of their wages. Managers believe that the corporation is not fulfilling its social mission unless it maintains employment. But it is sometimes impossible to keep an enterprise going unless it carries out layoffs. High compensation to laid-off employees is a sort of penalty imposed on an enterprise to keep it from carrying out layoffs as much as possible.

But even this system has limits. When a business situation deteriorates drastically, management, investors, and even creditors are held responsible. In the worst case large-scale personnel retrenchments, takeovers by another company, and dissolution of the company will be carried out. Of course the paternalistic nature of Japanese corporations would be meaningless if business conditions were allowed to slip to disastrous lows. It is important to observe where the threshold point lies and the margin of tolerance. Since smaller corporations have a smaller margin of tolerance than large ones, both labor and management try harder to keep their enterprises going with cooperative relationships.

The problems of paternalism are most clearly seen in the case of state-owned enterprises. The Japanese National Railways (JNR), for example, has continued to operate guided by its own internal logic in total disregard of objective circumstances. The result is a heavy financial burden on the nation as a whole.

Corporate Employees' Community

The corporate employees' community is knitted together by the ideology of company-based unions and stable employment. A corporate community exists in any enterprise in any country, but such a community is characterized somewhat differently in Japan. First, the regular male employees, who form the core of the community, are in the long-term service of the company and work continuously as a group. No differences in standing are felt among these employees though there exist gaps between the positions they occupy. Second, corporations as a whole, and employees as individuals, maintain little or no contact with outside organizations. Very few of the people in top management have been recruited from outside organizations, and most of those people have spent their entire career within a single corporation.

The fact that top management is not open to the influence of outside organizations is evident from the makeup of boards of directors. In Japan nearly 90 percent of the members of the boards of directors are also executives of the same companies—there are very few outside board members.

The existence of a corporate community can increase the vitality of the corporation and the will of employees to work. Such homogeneity promotes internal communications and often the improvement of business performance, but it can be a major weak point for corporations when their markets and technologies have reached a crossroads. In cases where markets are saturated or where business operations are technically deadlocked with managers experienced in nothing but outmoded products or technologies, the enterprises are late in altering behavior and often fail. Many Japanese industries—for example, cotton spinning, fertilizer, sugar refining, paper, and some chemical industries—find themselves in such a difficult situation because they have not adapted to industrial innovations.

In the United States outmoded enterprises customarily resort to mergers and acquisitions when they are attempting to find their way out of difficult circumstances. Business expansion through merger, however, is not common in Japan's industrial society. In Japan the use of financial power to take over what other corporations have laboriously created is considered to run counter to good business morality. But perhaps the more pragmatic reason is the virtually insurmountable difficulty of merging two closed exclusive communities into an efficient business organization.

Viewed from the investor's standpoint, the logic of corporations does not differ much in Japan from other countries. If business performance can be improved through merger, corporations throughout the world will aspire to amalgamation. In Japan, however, it is not easy to secure harmony between two different sets of corporate employees. In fact, if the consensus of the two employees' communities is not obtained, the merger is virtually impossible, even though the two boards of directors should vote for a merger. There are cases where a board of directors' decision on a business merger was canceled because of opposition by employees.

Generally, a corporation with a solid business performance merges with a corporation no longer able to survive through internal resources. To make the merger feasible, the stronger corporation completely absorbs the other corporation's community into its own. Although the fidelity of people to their corporate group is very high, when their corporation experiences bankruptcy, they are quite willing to cooperate fully with the takeover group in a new environment. Mergers, however, are exceedingly difficult to accomplish in Japan.

Decision Making by Top Management
Top management has two roles: administration of its corporate employees' community and enforcement of business operations through its organizational structure.

Administering people depends on solidifying a relationship between labor and management while fostering the willingness to work. This objective is achieved through employment security, impartial distribution of profits, and fair promotion of employees. Top management cannot hope to make any efficient decision unless reliable labor-management relations are established through the correct administration of the corporate employees' community.

On the one hand, top management's decision making involves the passive function of screening proposals presented by company staff after obtaining the in-company consensus, and, on the other, providing leadership to subordinates by delegating problems for them to solve. The latter is the more important activity. Top management in fact does not like to make formal decisions on proposals that are initially recommended by subordinates. It therefore follows certain complicated procedures before making a decision.

First, top management indicates its own ideas to the staff of the department presenting the proposals and requests the department to prepare implementing plans. Then top management has a responsible member of the department submit such plans to various meetings for review so that an in-company consensus on such plans can be shaped before final approval is given. In other words, top management endeavors to create an atmosphere conducive to the formation of the necessary corporate consensus.

When the proposals are ready to be implemented, not much time is wasted because working assignments have already been arranged. In a sense this decision-making formula responds to the willingness of subordinates to participate in management. In cases where there is no working harmony from the beginning, top management's decision-making job is extremely difficult.

Management's View of Daini Seikosha Multidivisional Operations

A corporation's continuation and development are aspirations common to both labor and management in Japan. We at Daini Seikosha have created an excellent management system in which the vitality of the enterprise and the employees' willingness to work interact. This management system, however, has many shortcomings insofar as strategic switchovers are concerned. Some of these problems may be enumerated as follows:

1. Because of exclusive labor-management relationships, negative reactions to what is outside the common experience.

2. Because of the confinement of all, including top management, within the corporate employees' community, lack of knowledge of the external environment.

3. Because of emphasis on employment maintenance by top management, difficulty in eliminating a nonprofit-making corporate division.

4. Because of great importance attached to the in-company consensus, difficulty in making effective decisions on how to conduct the multidivisional operations.

Daini Seikosha Co., Ltd. was an exclusive manufacturer of mechanical watches until about 1970 when it attempted to enter the machine-tool field. At that time many employees, though hardly all, felt that the watch market was reaching the saturation point. The company, after considerable discussion of how to cope with the great impending difficulties, decided to make a strategic switchover.

Also in 1970 we made public our long-range policy of expediting multidivisional business operations. This was not so much because we were afraid of possible saturation in the watch market as because the watchmaking techniques of our company were so special that they did not serve general purposes. The announcement of this long-range policy was further intended to make our employees acknowledge the willingness of the company to produce items other than timepieces.

The company then introduced technologies used in the electronic and scientific instruments industries. These new electronic and scientific instruments technologies had nothing directly to do with watchmaking; the company's objective was to expand technologies it already possessed. But it took much more time than we had imagined for such business operations to grow. This was not due to the paucity of synergy; rather, in the mid-1970s the momentum in the field had not yet been achieved. Nevertheless, we began producing electronic and quartz watches.

The company's failure to diversify was due too, in part, to the need for adequate management resources to implement the technological innovations. Yet these technological innovations brought about highly positive effects in our existing business operations.

Innovation in watch technologies was not aimed at enabling the watch industry to move into other industrial fields but was intended to revitalize watch production. Because of this we were able to set forth specific objectives and translate them into action without wasting too much time in preparation. In consequence Seiko has been able to take the initiative in the production of electronic wristwatches and thus to increase dramatically its share of the world market. Since our successful introduction of electronic wristwatches, we have begun to produce various kinds of electronic parts. A much longer time would have been spent in gearing up for these other multidivisional operations had we not made the technological incursions into watch production. With the ND Project, we hope to enable our company to make a radical technical departure from watchmaking and to market directly products in the new fields.

It may appear that the basic concept is so different from the Seiko Group's traditional structure that it may not win immediate in-company consensus. However, we have learned from earlier technological innovations and our experiences in the past recession that constant technological innovations are indispensable if we are to develop and expand employment. This has facilitated our employees' favorable response to the new concept.

We have set a current target of 7.5 percent in terms of before-tax profits, but we would like to achieve 10 percent or more. We have traditionally used this rate as our business goal.

The ND Project is currently at the stage where plans for the implementation of goals set by top management are being prepared at various divisions of the company and employees are being informed of the general strategy. The efforts toward multidivisional business operations have finally reached a turning point, and the ND Project's view has become accepted by all employees.

Conclusion

Japanese enterprises take it for granted that management-directed shifts in products are time-consuming. Yet, to ensure an early entry into a new line of activity, they must recognize external changes and move speedily to mobilize in-company resources. To affect such a change, there is a great need to include people in top management with business experiences outside the company.

In mobilizing in-company resources, it is important to divert the attention of managers from routine assignments to strategic planning. To attain this end, quality control circles can be adopted for strategic planning at a middle-management level. This will spur the creativity of those in middle management.

The problem confronting management is to maintain the efficient conduct of business, to secure and expand corporate profits and to distribute impartially and effectively the value that an enterprise generates to its employees. In this context the value is not necessarily limited to pay.

Once corporate employees agree to the need for new projects, the decision making begins with operational goals and plans. In the case where plans entirely new to an enterprise and its employees must be implemented, such as for multidivisional operations, there is a need to enlighten the corporate employees' community on the general strategy. The objective here lies in making every employee aware of the changes in the environment that have created the situation in which an enterprise is compelled to alter its course of operations. Without informing company employees about the strategic view, an enterprise cannot hope to obtain the cooperation of its subordinate organizations or expect it to formulate operational plans based on correct perspectives. Often the subordinate organization's staff is too busy with its routine assignments to grasp the actual situation in which the company is placed.

Lester Thurow
Reblending the American Economic Mixture

In a large corporation there are essentially two approaches to diversification and new products. The first is to plan the move from the top, with operating managers and workers taking the actions they have been ordered to take. The second approach is to work out a general corporate strategy and then convey it so clearly to the operating managers and workers that they will make the decisions top managers would have made if those top managers had been in their position. If it works, the aim of the second approach is to combine the strategic view of the top with the information available only to those in the field. The problem with the second approach is that it takes more time to convey the general strategy so that the field commanders will not make the wrong decisions.

In military terminology the issue is one of command and control. Consider the bombing issue in the Vietnam War. Do you pick bombing targets centrally at the Pentagon or convey the ultimate goals so clearly that the field commanders at the battle front can pick the right targets in a more flexible way than is ever possible from headquarters—but with the danger that they will pick the wrong target and bring the Chinese into the war?

If the first approach is chosen, the merger route is the most likely course for diversification. It is easier and quicker for the top management to acquire a going concern in the desired areas than it is to develop their own. This option is denied the Japanese manager, however; instead he must follow the in-house approach of trying to force rather than buy economic growth.

Although there are certainly examples of successful takeovers and mergers, the American corporate landscape is littered with the debris of unsuccessful efforts. Part of the problem may be that when firms can buy economic growth, management is never forced to become intimately involved with and knowledgeable about the business as they would if the growth had come internally. This tempts firms to move further away from their basic strengths—technology, marketing—than they can afford to move. For in the end it is not possible for good managers to manage anything. Detailed institutional and technological knowledge is usually necessary.

Seiko diversified, but only into products that were relevant to its basic market (from mechanical to electronic watches) or its basic technology (microelectronic production). In contrast, American firms tend to act as if management is a general skill and industry-specific knowledge is not necessary or can easily be acquired. In the 1960s the American steel industry, for instance, was run by financiers who knew little or nothing about steel technology. Given this ignorance, it fell behind in the revolution that led to oxygen furnaces and continuous casting. The industry is now trying to solve its failures in the steel business by getting out of it and into unrelated businesses such as oil. It is too early to judge whether this will be a success, but there is clearly room for skepticism based on past performance. What might have happened if steel managers knew that both as firms and individuals they would economically fail or succeed depending on their ability to run a world-class steel operation? I suspect that America today would have more viable materials firms.

The American mixture needs to be reblended to make the quick merger and takeover less available. Instant success is not likely by this route, but the mirage of instant success seemingly offered distracts from the real task of building new successful industries.

7

Strategy for Overseas Markets

Takashi "Tachi" Kiuchi

The Mitsubishi Electric Corporation employs 48,000 persons, 680 engaged directly in work related to overseas operations. Three hundred persons work abroad at sixty-four firms scattered in thirty-one countries. The company, founded in 1920, manufactures electronics and electric machinery and appliances.

Mitsubishi Electric can be described as an enterprise trying to get rid of outdated traditions built up over its history. In early 1982, as a result of a reshuffle of its management, the company's overseas operations, ranging from electric home appliances to semiconductors, electronic systems, industrial machinery and equipment, and heavy electric equipment, were placed under the control of one group led by a single leader.

Establishment of Long-Range Goals

"What vision do you have for the Japanese society or the world in the year 1990 or 1999?" asked the leader of the overseas operations group. Twenty-eight senior employees, department chiefs with many years of work experience abroad, gathered to discuss this subject. They all recognized that a continuation of the old ways of conducting business would not benefit the company. Those companies that fail are companies dependent on their past achievements, whose employees expect things to improve without effort, where bad or unwelcome news is hard to spread but where good news is exaggerated, where employees believe that they have nothing to worry about because everybody is working hard like worker-bees. Finally, everyone believed that their company had no guiding philosophy and little experience putting new ideas into practice. They hoped their discussion, conducted from a long-range and world-wide perspective, would result in establishing a strategy with a long-range vision.

World Situation

It may be impossible to predict the future, but one thing is certain: there always will be conflicts among nations. The usual tensions may be complicated by problems relating to hegemony and population growth, and shortages of food, energy, and other resources. An aging population will also exacerbate the welfare problem.

At the same time there can be positive developments. Technological advances may open up entirely new opportunities for business. Increases in our standards of living may bring about changes in human philosophy, desires, sense of values, and taste. Therefore business, if it wishes to survive fierce international competition, will need to develop bold new strategies.

Future Overseas Strategy

First, the meeting participants, all members of the overseas operations group, concluded steps should be taken to increase the managerial consciousness of its employees on overseas assignments that overseas success depended on the pursuit of profits. Second, they focused on problems with the company's system of recruiting and promoting. In what was a radical step for a Japanese company they decided to recruit foreigners in an effort to find employees with different backgrounds and different blood.

Third, they challenged the company's previous decision to manufacture and sell abroad but to leave research and development to the home base. To develop products that meet the needs of overseas markets it will be necessary to conduct research free from Japan's traditional and inherent restrictions. Because Mitsubishi Electric's corporate climate is hostile to new products, the participants saw a need to form a special group that would promote the growth of new products in overseas markets. Takeovers of foreign enterprises, joint ventures with foreign businesses, and new ventures are important constituents of the new overseas strategy.

Other problems discussed included the need to cultivate experts in international financial matters, to withdraw from products and business with a poor competitive position and little future potential, to transfer more power to overseas affiliated firms, and to induce employees assigned abroad to remain there for longer periods of time.

Large-scale changes will occur in the 1990s and will open up new business opportunities. Those who wish to survive in the fierce competitive struggle ahead will find that educational background and social or economic position will become less important and that the ability and volition of the individual will play a greater role in the survival of the company. Each employee must consider how he or she can contribute to the company. Each must have new ideas and the determination and leadership to take chances.

Strategically, emphasis will be placed on areas that promise rapid growth and areas that have the advantage of scarcity value.

Structure of Overseas Operations

In the past exports played a comparatively minor role in our business. They were regarded as a way for businesses to deal with saturated domestic markets and surplus production capacity. It goes without saying that in those days domestic and overseas markets existed separately in the minds of our managers.

Today the situation is different. The domestic market is now part of the world market. Production for domestic markets and production for exports play equally important roles in a large corporation. Management now must meet the challenge of starting local production abroad, establishing sales channels as close as possible to the ultimate consumers, and undertaking foreign projects on a turnkey basis. These changes will inevitably transform the structure of overseas business operations.

Headquarters
In the past each group of Mitsubishi Electric's products had a trade section in charge of exports. Overseas strategies were developed for each product. For example, the heavy machinery group had a heavy machinery overseas marketing division which in turn had overseas bases under its control. Today, however, a different way of thinking prevails.

The organization has been undergoing changes for the following reasons: (1) the need to avoid organizational overlap, (2) the need to give a greater power to those who head the foreign bases, (3) the need to integrate international finance into overseas operations, (4) the need, as more and more of Mitsubishi Electric's business has become related to electronics, to reorganize around electronics, and (5) the need to integrate software and civil engineering operations as they become more important aspects of business.

As a result of these changes the company's overseas operations have been placed under the single command of the International Operations Group. No longer will overseas strategy be discussed merely in its relationship to domestic business or influenced by the operating capacity of the products division. Now our overseas strategy can be worked out on the basis of a time span of ten or twenty years and operated independently.

In several years many Japanese companies will move their overseas operations headquarters to foreign countries. If they continue to stay in Japan, a local market, they will find it impossible to understand the world market and to recruit needed employees.

Overseas Organization

To be successful, an overseas organization must gain a firm footing in the major markets of the world and be accepted by each local community. It should establish overseas marketing bases, production bases, and technology centers — in that order. Finally, the umbrella company that controls all of these activities should be given financial control.

Those in charge of overseas operations should be instructed to reach the break-even point three years after the establishment of the local bases, eliminate deficits in five years, and begin paying dividends in seven years — although these targets will vary according to regional differences and product type. Also overseas operations should be told never to forget three no's. Never get involved in legal issues, never allow the formation of labor unions, and never fail to collect accounts receivable.

Each overseas base should be free to develop the means necessary to achieve the goals set by the parent company. Each should decide on finance and sales policies, quantities and kinds of products using flexible manufacturing systems, and whether to place tenders or accept orders for turnkey projects. If the overseas affiliates are too strongly influenced by conditions and capacities in Japan, they will not become welcome enterprises in foreign markets nor motivate local employees to work their level best.

Supporting Structure

Company staff groups—public relations, law, personnel, controllers, finance, purchasing, publicity, and technology development—are important for international operations and should participate in foreign efforts. Since our company is located in Japan with tens of thousands of employees engaged in domestic activities, the information available to staff groups comes overwhelmingly from domestic sources. Managing directors' meetings and board meetings have an important role to play in improving this situation. The speech and conduct of the president and other chief executive officers can have an important bearing on how foreign operations are viewed.

With the establishment of Mitsubishi Electric's Overseas Operating Group, three staffs—Overseas Planning and Administration, Overseas Financing and Accounting, and Overseas Affiliate Operations—will direct their attention to overseas operations and attempt to make the main office's overall policies sensitive to the needs of overseas operations. The most important problems are to secure talented employees, to raise funds for starting business abroad, and to promote the development of new products for overseas markets.

The products group will start off with the handicap of being regarded as merely another outlet for products developed for domestic markets. To counter this, every section of the products group must have employees whose main responsibilities are overseas operations. The technological division in charge of engineering, development, and design must have staff who understand what overseas markets need and who are well versed in foreign languages and have experience abroad. Finally, the products group must accept methods and traditions prevailing in foreign countries. The United States and Europe have many technologies, and methods, not used in Japan that can provide surprising results when combined with the Japanese way of doing things.

Tasks

The most important task in promoting overseas operations is to enable our people to maintain their determination to be successful. Just as Americans lost their desire in the late 1960s, the Japanese seem to be growing self-complacent. Only when employees are dedicated to the goal of maintaining high productivity growth will they maintain their competitive position in world markets.

Japanese corporations have a major problem in efficiently employing foreigners in that it is very difficult to integrate them into the traditional management structure. In the past Japanese corporations had a strong competitive position in the price and quality of their products and conducted their own sales activities. Today as local purchases and production increase, Japanese companies cannot expect their growth to continue without cooperation with major foreign corporations. Under such circumstances it has become necessary to hire experienced foreigners.

Problems Facing Electronics and Electric Machinery and Appliances Industry

A number of problems confront Japan's electric machinery and appliances industry:

1. *Worldwide recession*   Increasing resistance to foreign trade is working against the export of Japanese durable consumer goods, and excessive debts of developing countries are causing a decrease in the number of plants Japanese companies can afford to buy. The problem is exacerbated by more restrictions on Japanese exports, a rising demand for overseas production, and the need for active cooperation with U.S. and European manufacturers.

2. *Deceleration of domestic economic expansion*   The demand for heavy machinery and industrial products has declined

within Japan, and the structure for consumer goods demand has changed.

3. *Rapid changes in the use of electronics* There has been rapid progress in foreign countries in the science of semiconductors, numerical controls, robotics, computers, and space communication.

4. *Development of new energy sources* Research and development on fuel cells and machinery utilizing solar energy are new trends that threaten Japan's electric industry.

Companies will find it difficult to cope with any of these problems unless they mobilize all of their personnel, money, goods, and information. To solve these problems, the help of trading companies will be necessary. At the present time it seems possible that the cooperative relationship that prevailed between trading companies and manufacturers thirty years ago will be revived.

Relationship with Trading Companies

Since 1945 manufacturing and trading companies have been mutually strengthening and supplementing each other's functions. In the electronics and electric machinery and equipment industries, however, manufacturers have now become independent of the trading companies in their export activities.

And since the first oil crisis in 1973 trading companies began to seek new roles. Breaking from their traditional role as merchants or wholesalers in the distribution sector, they have begun to play the role of investor, especially as developers of natural resources. As trading firms strengthened the political activities necessary to protect their investments, manufacturers simultaneously strengthened their marketing of mass-produced goods, though they still use trading companies for the export of plant machinery.

Now manufacturers and trading companies are once again cooperating with each other. The days when manufacturers could enjoy automatic growth because of the fast growth of the Japanese economy are now over. On world markets opposition to trade seems to be growing in parallel with the deterioration in general economic conditions in the United States and Europe. The need to cope with trade resistance is likely to engender cooperation between manufacturers and trading companies.

Our task as a firm is to acquire the capacity to be a world enterprise. The first job for manufacturers is to utilize efficiently their resources—personnel, money, organization, goods, and information. The second is to expand each of their overseas operations, from sales to servicing, production, and research. The third job is to develop new electronic products and to create new businesses, first in the United States and then in Europe. Finally, qualitative improvement rather than quantitative considerations should be given top priority. This task must become the objective of other manufacturers as well.

From the trading companies, manufacturers expect the following:

1. *Abundant personal contacts*   Trading companies have strong close relationships with leaders of foreign countries and major corporations, often a closer relationship than that held by the Japanese government. Manufacturers generally lack such contacts.

2. *Information*   Manufacturers are likely to seek markets only in related industries. In contrast, trading companies maintain relationships with a full range of primary, secondary, and tertiary industries, enabling them to grasp a picture of world markets based on information gathered from various sources.

3. *Development*   Trading companies should perform the important function of developer in creating national projects and in finding or promoting large-scale private projects. This should go beyond traditional power supply projects.

4. *Finance* Trading companies have a great advantage in finance. As a result of the increased recognition of Japan's industrial power, electric machinery manufacturers often receive proposals for investment in overseas production or generate such proposals themselves. The number of cases requiring large investment is increasing. The trading companies' financing and credibility will be useful in this area.

5. *Function of mutual trading* As trade restrictions become more common, the trading companies' role as an importer of primary products becomes extremely important. It is very difficult for manufacturers to solve the problem of counterpurchases demanded by communist, socialist, and developing countries. This is a function trading companies can perform.

Trading companies can help in solving each of these problems facing manufacturers. The problem revolves around the long-range outlook if trading companies will bring to bear the risks involved in these new undertakings.

International Friction

International friction is unavoidable under the free trade system. Today while the world economy continues its sluggish growth, Japanese companies are likely to step up export efforts, forgetting the bitter lessons learned from past experiences. After a thirty-year effort to expand exports, Japan must now seriously tackle the problem of maintaining economic growth while mitigating friction.

As Japan has rapidly expanded its exports by sharpening its competitive edge, the inevitable result has been international friction. In the 1950s and 1960s problems arose in light-industry products such as textiles, cameras, telescopes, sewing machines, and bicycles; in the 1970s the export of color televisions, autos, shipbuilding, and steel led to restrictions; today semiconductors, numerical con-

trolled machine tools, and industrial machinery are leading to pressures for restriction. In the 1980s and 1990s
similar problems may occur concerning high-technology
products such as computers, aircraft, robotics, and drugs.

International competitiveness encompasses a variety of
factors. In addition to price there are nonprice factors such
as quality, performance, date of delivery, and service. But
basically Japan's rising competitiveness has been due to the
rate of growth in its labor productivity which has been
higher than that of other countries. To some extent the
growth in labor productivity has been caused by high plant
and equipment investment, but it has also been influenced
by technological innovation, favorable labor-management
relationships, and a superior labor force.

Behind the decline of vitality in the United States lies the
growth of complex regulations and labor union power.
Both excessive regulations and excessive union power
push up prices and obstruct national, corporate, and individual power. Japan, to the contrary, is not a law-ori-
ented society, and its labor unions do not exercise great
influence.

Japan is heavily influenced by Buddhist thought, the
teaching of Confucius, and an acceptance of the uncertainty of life. These factors explain the Japanese people's
diligence, their willingness to save, their strong inclination
to know foreign things, their capability to adjust to a
changing world, their spirit of harmony which gives priority to the maintenance of order in their communities and
organizations, and their way of regarding their relationship with other members of a group. Here lies the source of
our strong international competitive position. And with it
the inevitable problem of international friction.

The U.S. and European economies do not seem to have
recovered from the impact of the oil crises. Prices still continue to rise, and the tight-money measures effectuated to
contain inflation have touched off a sharp rise in interest
rates and a decline in domestic demand. As a result slug-

gish plant and equipment investment has caused a deterioration in competitiveness affecting employment and the trade balance. Worse, the United States and Europe have adopted passive economic and industrial revitalization policies designed to maintain the status quo and to prevent their present profits from dropping. They should shed their perfectionist attitude of avoiding competition and encourage industries to develop new products or to shift to other fields of endeavor.

Solutions for International Friction

When we consider measures to counter international friction, we should regard the following facts. The world economy will never regain the fast pace of growth it had in the recent past. Energy prices, foreign exchange fluctuations, and interest rates exert such an influence that business conditions change at the same time everywhere in the world. Because the free trade system is an important common property, the system must be maintained, with all countries sharing the costs of maintaining it.

We at Mitsubishi Electric have formulated some measures to solve international friction and have been making efforts to enact them. Before touching on them, it is important to confirm the following points of contention. First, trade imbalances have emerged not because Japan has forcibly exported but because people abroad have been willing to buy superior but cheap goods. Second, all major cases of trade friction are made the subject of Japan's voluntary export restriction or of the importing country's import restriction. Third, foreign requests concerning Japan's nontariff trade barriers are tantamount to raising objections to Japan's social structure. Therefore there is little possibility that those requests will be met.

Mitsubishi Electric has been advocating the following measures in an effort to solve the friction:

1. *Maximum reliance on local employees* Efforts should be made to fill as many posts as possible in overseas operations with local employees. Even at the headquarters and plants in Japan development of products for U.S. markets and decision making on their marketing policy should be entirely left to Americans.

2. *Construction of manufacturing plants near places where demand is high* With the development of flexible manufacturing systems, it is possible to produce many kinds of products in small quantities at competitive prices without mass producing a particular product. As marketing bases are located in each market, so too engineering centers and manufacturing plants must be located in each country and market.

3. *Cooperation with major companies abroad* There are too many electronics and electric machinery and appliances companies today. I believe that the number of such companies in the world will fall to fourteen groups in ten years. To remain within one of the fourteen groups, Mitsubishi Electric should expand its business through cooperation with a leading electronics and electric machinery company. Unless outdated laws such as the antitrust act are amended as soon as possible, industries of countries with such restrictions will lose out.

Japanese Enterprises and National Boundaries
The domestic market is a local sector of the world market. Mitsubishi Electric is trying to gain a firm footing in more than one hundred local markets in the world and to become a company whose existence can be justified in each market. As shown by the video cassette recorder, it is possible to perceive what each overseas market demands and to meet that demand by discriminating among products, individualizing them, and improving their quality. By so doing, we can have our products willingly accepted by local

markets despite competition from semideveloped and developing countries.

Guidelines for Colleagues Working Abroad
As an example of what I have stated so far, I will introduce a written appeal recently mailed by the company to the 300 resident employees engaged in overseas operations.

1. People working abroad are given a rare opportunity to break away from the traditional Japanese way of doing business and become businessmen who can be accepted anywhere in the world.

2. Many overseas affiliates bear a name different from that of the holding company in Japan. This may sometimes pose a problem in conducting business. Viewed from a different angle, however, this provides employees an opportunity to be accepted on their own merits without the weight of the parent company behind them.

3. Salesmen and engineers assigned abroad may concentrate so much on communication with the headquarters in Japan that they neglect their basic role. Communication with the head office in Japan is important, but those who neglect local affairs will find themselves squeezed out of local markets.

4. Engineers and salesmen should conduct themselves confidently in front of customers and speak in an impressive manner. They must be sensitive and refrain from smoking in front of nonsmoking customers.

5. Those engaged in production in Japan must seriously realize that products of other companies may be selling well because of superior quality. Salesmen working abroad must seriously realize that the products of other companies may be selling well because other salesmen for those companies are more adept in sales.

6. Employees must keep a close watch on other companies, if necessary, spending money for that purpose.

They should have plans and strategies to win over rivals, not be satisfied with moderate efforts or strategies designed merely to give results equal to those of other companies or to improve business slightly compared with the preceding year.

7. Nobody will buy goods from a person who can barely manage to explain his products in the language of customers. Employees must master the necessary foreign languages.

8. Make the most of the company's purchasing power. There are people in charge of purchases at the company's overseas production and marketing bases scattered throughout the world. Do our salesmen know how much of what products they purchase from what companies? You ought to sell something to those companies.

9. Employees must always pay attention to colleagues' performances, particularly when those colleagues are of different nationality or different racial backgrounds. You will never fail to learn from them.

10. Nothing will stymie our utmost efforts to encourage the enthusiasm of our colleagues working in the forefront abroad.

Lester Thurow
Reblending the American Economic Mixture

Given the time that it takes to break into major foreign markets, it is clear that a long time horizon is essential for any firm that seeks to become a major multinational company. In countries where you cannot buy already existing firms, it is not possible to become a major presence quickly or to earn instant profits. But a long horizon is useless unless it is linked with a long-run strategic view of the future. What is the world going to be like ten to twenty years in the future? Where do you want your firm to be at that time?

How do these strategic goals become specific firm goals and affect specific project goals?

According to Kiuchi, Mitsubishi Electric starts with a long-range view of what people want and then attempts to figure out what products flow from these wants. This list of potential products is then combed to find those products that fit in with Mitsubishi Electric's comparative advantage. The specific goal is to become one of *Fortune* magazine's ten largest companies within that ten- to twenty-year horizon. Normally individual products are expected to start generating net profits within seven years.

When it comes to exporting, probably the major change required in American behavioral patterns is a willingness to be patient and a willingness to study foreign markets to determine what foreigners want. Datsun, for example, is rumored to have lost money in the American market for ten years before it started to generate profits. Such patience is required if you are going to break into major markets where there are entrenched strong local producers such as Ford or General Motors. A major market such as autos cannot be conquered quickly.

Even more important, however, is a willingness to study what foreigners want. The first Japanese cars were failures in the American market because they were cars designed for the Japanese market rather than for the American market. American firms have often been successful exporters but almost always because they happened to be making a product for the American market that the rest of the world wanted but could not make itself because it lacked the necessary technology. Seldom do we design products specifically for foreign markets. But now that our huge post-World War II technological lead has evaporated, there are going to be fewer and fewer products that we can export simply because we, and no one else, have the technology necessary to make the products. Combine this with an economy that has become increasingly dependent on imports and exports, and you have a mixture of cir-

cumstances that will force major changes in American behavioral patterns if we wish to remain economically successful.

Essentially the American problem is the reverse of the
one described by Kiuchi. Japanese companies such as
Mitsubishi Electric have to learn how to become multinational companies with production and research facilities
around the world. American companies have to learn how
to export when they do not possess a technologically
unique product. As Kiuchi recognizes, neither is easy to do.

But it has to be done since the industrial leaders of the
1990s are likely to be those firms that have a strong international base and not those firms that are limited to their
home market. When the American home market was 50
percent of the world GNP after World War II, a firm could
be satisfied with a strong position in the American market
and could ignore the rest of the world. As the American
GNP shrinks relative to the rest of the world (the American
GNP is now less than the Common Market's GNP), such a
position becomes less and less tenable if a firm wants to
remain successful.

8

Competition and Cooperation among Japanese Corporations

Munemichi Inoue

The Japanese economy has grown rapidly over the past thirty years. And although the rate of growth began to decline in the 1970s, it has continued to stay at a high level compared with other advanced industrial nations.

Various factors produced the rapid growth of the Japanese economy, but the driving force was competition. Competition has led corporations to strive for technological and managerial innovations. Amid keen competition, which has often been labeled excessive competition, Japanese corporations have made an effort to introduce technology and expand their markets, thus producing rapid economic growth.

Although competing intensely, corporations nevertheless have maintained cooperation among themselves. Limitations on the availability of funds and managerial know-how have led to efforts to overcome these limitations through cooperation. A corporation, for example, that lacks experience in overseas operations and has only limited capital will face difficulties in developing and importing resources independently. What is particularly notable in this situation is the existence of industrial groups. Big corporations in mining and manufacturing, finance, and commerce form industrial groups through a unique relationship of cooperation not found in other countries.

Present Industrial Groups

The Japanese industrial groups today have their origin in the *zaibatsu*, which were disbanded following the end of World War II. A *zaibatsu* was a pyramid-type business enterprise in which a holding company owned by a wealthy family controlled various business enterprises, which in turn controlled many subsidiaries and affiliated firms. Activities within the group were placed under the firm grip of the holding company, which acted as the supreme headquarters, and member companies had to maintain a relationship of close cooperation with each other.

Four *zaibatsu*—Mitsui, Mitsubishi, Sumitomo, and Yasuda—were particularly strong in the Japanese economy. At the end of World War II they accounted for a quarter of the nation's total paid-in capital. At that time there were also seven newly established *zaibatsu* and sixteen smaller localized *zaibatsu*.

The present industrial groups were born with those *zaibatsu* as a background. Today there are six big industrial groups, three springing from former *zaibatsu* (table 8.1). Although the present industrial groups have historical relationships with the former *zaibatsu*, they are basically different from the *zaibatsu* in three ways.

First, the former *zaibatsu* centered on commercial power (particularly general trading companies), whereas the present industrial groups are based on financial power. General trading companies still play an important role in the present industrial groups, but the central role is played by financial institutions. Big banks, trust banks, life insurance companies, and property insurance companies participate in the industrial groups and provide funds for member companies.

Table 8.1
Time and formation of presidents' groups and number of member companies

Former *zaibatsu*	Name	Time of formation	Number of member firms
Mitsui	Nimoku-kai	1961	23
Mitsubishi	Mitsubishi Kinyo-kai	1955	28
Sumitomo	Hakusui-kai	1951–1952	21
Banks			
Fuji	Fuyo-kai	1966	29
Sanwa	Sansui-kai	1967	39
Dai-ichi Kang in	Sankin-kai	1978	45

Note: As of July 1, 1979, Hitachi, Ltd., belongs to both Fuji and Sanwa groups. Nippon Express Co., Ltd., belongs to both Dai-ichi Kangin and Sanwa presidents' groups.

Second, member companies groups are more independent in decision making. In the former *zaibatsu* the holding companies had an important role in planning investments. With the present industrial groups, however, each member company independently makes decisions. A presidents' group (composed of the presidents of an industrial group) merely plays a mediating role, serving as a forum for exchanging information or as a study meeting for participants. Such groups try to create a consensus among member firms on participation in big projects, but the decision as to whether to participate is left to the judgments of the individual companies.

Third, each member of an industrial group conducts business transactions with nonmember companies, and this business constitutes most of their business. This is related to the decentralization of decision making. The decision as to whether to purchase raw materials or machinery is made on the basis of price. Purchases are made from member companies if the desired goods are offered at lower prices than those of nonmember companies, but goods are also purchased from nonmember companies if their prices are more competitive.

General trading companies play an important role in transactions among member companies, but their sales to member firms of the same industrial group account for only about 5 percent of their total sales. Member companies' transactions with the general trading company of the same industrial group account for less than 30 percent of their total sales or purchases.

These facts show that the present industrial groups differ in character from the former *zaibatsu*. Compared with the tight unity of the *zaibatsu*, they are more loosely united.

Industrial Groups and Means of Cooperation

The present industrial groups are loosely united, but they have several means of maintaining their cooperative relationships. The means for maintaining unity include stock ownership, financial relations, concurrent holding of executive posts in two or more companies, executive exchanges with other member firms, and other business tie-ups.

Mutual stock ownership is the traditional means of maintaining strong stockholders. When member companies did not yet have adequate technology and managerial know-how, they tried to secure strong stockholders to avoid takeovers through mutual stock ownership.

The following two points are notable. First, in the present industrial groups no single member company exhibits a particularly high ratio of stock ownership in the other members of the group. The unity of the industrial groups is maintained, rather, through mutual stock ownership of member companies at a comparatively low rate. In three major industrial groups the mutual ownership rates as of 1979 were 14.9 percent for Mitsui, 24.1 percent for Mitsubishi, and 25.7 percent for Sumitomo.

Second, corporations are inclined to invest in areas with favorable financial yields and refrain from holding stocks merely for the sake of ownership. As a result even the need to secure strong stockholders has been conditional as corporations have been trying to avoid inefficient stock investments. However, since the interlocking stockholdings have contributed to the stabilization of stock prices, the system brings benefits to its members other than helping them to control other firms (see tables 8.2 and 8.3).

On the other hand, the financial relationship between member group banks and group companies differs from that of mutual stock ownership because the relationship between the banks and other companies is one-sided rather than reciprocal. During the period of high economic growth corporations faced the problem of how to raise funds. Under such circumstances member firms were in a comparatively advantageous position. When their business deteriorated, particularly during a period of recession, member companies were in a better position than nonmembers to seek relief from the main banks associated with their group.

Table 8.2
Ratio of interlocking stockholdings (percent)

Average for three groups of *zaibatsu* origin	Average for three bank-affiliated groups	Average for six groups
28.35	18.23	23.29

Source: The Fair Trade Commission of the Japanese Government, A Survey on the Industrial Groupings of Japan.
Note: Actual figures for fiscal 1977 based on securities reports filed by companies. Figures represent those of industrial group member companies listed on securities exchanges and those of life insurance companies. Interlocking ratio is

$$\frac{\frac{\text{Total stocks held vs.}}{\text{total stocks issued by industrial group}}}{\text{Number of companies in each group}} \times 100.$$

Table 8.3
Stockholdings according to industries

	Average for three groups of *zaibatsu* origin	Average for three bank-affiliated groups	Average for six groups
Banks	28.50	37.74	32.12
Life insurance	18.59	16.51	17.78
Property insurance	7.69	3.79	6.14
Trading companies	7.90	7.02	7.56
Mining	1.69	0	1.03
Construction	1.67	1.76	1.12
Manufacturing	30.62	31.60	31.00
Commerce	0.04	0.02	0.08
Real estate	2.54	0.16	1.63
Transportation, communication	1.62	1.15	1.46
Service, other	0.14	0.05	0.08
Total	100	100	100

Note: Actual figures for fiscal 1977. Figures represent those of industrial group member companies listed on securities exchanges and those of life insurance companies. Based on securities reports filed by companies. Stockholding ratio according to industrial

category is $\dfrac{\text{Total stocks held by companies in industrial group vs. total stocks issued by group}}{\text{Number of companies in each group}} \times 100.$

Although financial ties within industrial groups were one-sided relationships, it should be noted that the principle of competition played an effective role in the Japanese money market. According to a Fair Trade Commission survey on industrial groups, the ratio of industrial group member companies' borrowing from the banks within the same group to their total debts in fiscal 1977 averaged 24.49 percent for the three groups with origins in the former *zaibatsu,* 18.05 percent for the other three groups, and 21.27 percent for the six groups.

The ratio has been declining since it reached a peak in 1960, for two reasons. First, during the period of high economic growth, many nonmember companies were

Table 8.4
Rate of dependence on borrowing within industrial groups

	Average for three groups of *zaibatsu* origin	Average for three bank-affiliated groups	Average for six groups
Long-term borrowing	23.76	14.61	19.19
Short-term borrowing	25.87	24.01	24.94
Total	24.49	18.05	21.27

Note: Actual figures for fiscal 1977 based on securities reports filed by companies. Figures represent those of industrial group member companies listed on securities exchanges and those of life insurance companies. Ratio of dependence on borrowing within

industrial groups is $\dfrac{\text{Borrowing from banks within group}}{\text{Total borrowing by member companies}} \times 100.$

growing rapidly and the banks within industrial groups actively lent to those nonmember companies. Because the financial institutions are also private companies, they directed their funds to areas with good yields.

Second, member companies have chosen an independent course of management and have deliberately refrained from excessive dependence on member banks. These companies wanted to avoid the psychological dependence resulting from excessive reliance on one particular financial institution. Diversifying their borrowings also helped them to gain access to nonmember companies through other banks (see table 8.4).

Human ties also serve as a means of strengthening cooperation. This takes the form of executives concurrently holding posts in two or more companies or of companies dispatching their executives to other companies. There are two factors leading to such exchanges. One is the transfer of managerial know-how. When an employee with outstanding managerial capability moves to a different company, managerial know-how moves with him. The transfer of managerial know-how is not popular in Japan but is gradually increasing.

Table 8.5
Percentage of executives from other companies within the same
industrial group

	Average for three groups of *zaibatsu* origin	Average for three bank-affiliated groups	Average for six groups
Percentage of executives coming from other companies	10.54	6.04	8.29
Percentage of companies with executives from other companies within same group	71.22	60.07	65.64
Of the above, percentage of companies with executives from banks	62.05	48.96	55.51

Note: Figures represent executives coming from other companies
within the same groups who have become board members since 1955.
Figures also represent those of industrial group member companies
listed on securities exchanges and those of life insurance companies, based on securities reports filed by companies. Percentage of
executives coming from other companies within the same industrial

$$\text{group is } \frac{\text{Total executives from other companies within same industrial group}}{\text{Total executives in each industrial group}} \times 100. \text{ Percentage}$$

of companies having executives from other companies with same

$$\text{group is } \frac{\text{Total companies with executives from other companies within same group}}{\text{Number of member companies of each group}} \times 100.$$

Another is the creation of channels of information.
There are various ways to communicate information. The
transfer of a person often enables better communication
of information, particularly in Japan where human relationships are emphasized. Communicating information
through the transfer of employees is an important managerial strategy in Japan.

According to a Fair Trade Commission survey, board
members concurrently hold executive posts in two or more
member companies at the rate of three or four per 100

Table 8.6
Ratio of executives concurrently holding executive posts

	Average for three groups of *zaibatsu* origin	Average for three bank-affiliated groups	Average for six groups
Percentage of executives concurrently holding executive posts	3.58	1.81	2.70
Percentage of companies with executives concurrently holding posts in two or more companies	38.30	19.20	28.75

Note: Actual figures for fiscal 1977. Figures represent those of industrial group member companies listed on securities exchanges and those of life insurance companies, based on securities reports filed by companies. Percentage of concurrent holding of executive posts is

$$\text{tive posts is } \frac{\text{Total executives with posts in two or more companies within same group}}{\text{Total executives of each industrial group}} \times 100.$$

Percentage of companies having executives concurrently holding posts in two or more companies is

$$\frac{\text{Number of companies accepting executives from other companies within same group}}{\text{Number of member companies of each industrial group}} \times 100.$$

executives. About 70 percent of the companies belonging to the same three industrial groups also have board members coming from other member companies (see tables 8.5 and 8.6).

In both cases executives from financial institutions share a majority of the concurrent executive posts as well as dispatch a greater number of executives to other firms, reflecting the fact that the present-day industrial groups are increasing their dependence on financial institutions.

However, it usually takes a lot of time for executives holding posts in different member firms to have their merits recognized in each company. Although the social climate is more open than it used to be, human ties are still decisive in Japanese business management, and it takes several years for executives dispatched to different member companies to get along well with people of their new companies.

Joint ventures are another means of cooperation. Joint ventures are seen more frequently among member companies of an industrial group than between member and nonmember companies.

A Fair Trade Commission survey conducted in 1976 on joint ventures covering 809 nonfinancial companies listed on the Tokyo Securities Exchange and 36 other major nonfinancial companies found the following to be true:

1. Only 17 percent of the 845 companies surveyed were members of industrial groups, but 50 percent of the surveyed companies said that they had signed joint venture agreements.

2. Joint ventures are signed not only between group members but also between member and nonmember companies; however, joint ventures are much more frequent between member companies.

3. Cases of joint ventures are more frequent between members of industrial groups of *zaibatsu* origin.

4. Of the joint ventures between member companies, such ventures accounted for more than 50 percent of total joint ventures, and technological agreements were the next most significant type of joint ventures.

5. In the industrial groups of *zaibatsu* origin, general trading companies have entered into joint ventures with other member companies, playing the role of organizer within the group.

Joint ventures mean the further strengthening of cooperative relations within industrial groups, and recently joint ventures with nongroup member companies have been increasing. Behind this increase has been the desire of individual companies to strengthen ties with their most advantageous partners, particularly in carrying out large overseas projects.

Factors for New Group Formation

Several corporations in Japan have formed, though conditionally, industrial groups and are trying to maintain cooperative relationships. There are three reasons most commonly put forth.

First, transaction costs are saved through the formation of industrial groups. By serving as a communication club, member companies can reduce their costs of obtaining information on technology, markets, and general social or economic situations.

The advantage of this arrangement becomes clear when viewed from each of three perspectives—when each corporation behaves independently, when all corporations behave as a merged single organization, and when corporations loosely associated in present industrial groups and member companies are assured of independent decision making.

In the first instance companies are exposed to the uncertainty and risks of collecting information and conducting transactions and, in so doing, must bear high costs. Such costs would be particularly enormous in international transactions. In the second instance transaction costs will be sharply reduced because all transactions are carried out within the same organization, but new costs will result from organizational efficiency and deficiency of scale. Incentives to innovation may become weaker in a big organization. In the third instance companies have a greater advantage in terms of costs than companies in the second instance because they are assured of independence.

Second, there is a limit to the managerial ability found in corporations. Or it may be more appropriate to say that there has been a limit to the managerial ability of Japanese companies. In the management of Japanese companies the process of decision making has usually been bottom up. Only rarely do top executives themselves devise a strategy or policy. While bottom-top decision making has been frequent with big business, top-bottom decision making has been more frequent with many small companies.

Top executives have had to increase their managerial ability through cooperation with their counterparts in other companies. There has been a limit to their managerial ability, particularly in international transactions involving the development and importing of resources, the introduction of technology, and the development of new markets. In order to keep pace with corporate growth, Japanese corporations have acquired greater managerial ability, but the limitations of managerial ability have been a problem until recently.

Third, the formation of industrial groups reduces the cost of funds because of the institutional characteristics of Japanese money markets. Discretional credit allocation has been a common practice in Japan's long-term money markets. In short-term money markets a low interest rate policy has been maintained to prevent interest rates from rising sharply. These policies were maintained at least until the first half of the 1970s and lead to nonprice credit rationing.

Because of these institutional characteristics both long-term and short-term funds have been allocated according to the size of a corporation, and therefore larger companies have had comparatively greater bargaining power vis-à-vis financial institutions. Furthermore the larger the industrial group, the more bargaining power it had vis-à-vis the government. Indeed, the size of the corporation has been important in securing funds and reducing the costs of funds.

On the other hand, financial institutions have had difficulties collecting on loans. An important problem for them has been securing guarantees for loans to companies with unfavorable capital structures and uncertain futures.

As a result financial institutions have lent to member companies through general trading companies rather than directly, essentially hedging against risks by securing guarantees from the general trading companies. It has been possible to keep the cost of funds comparatively low because of the hedge against risks implicit in the loans.

Today the cost of funds and the limitation of managerial ability are not as important in the formation of industrial groups.

Japanese corporations act in order to maximize their sales and to gain the greatest possible profits. This motive is behind the formation of industrial groups and company participation in such groups. The main factors behind group formation are the reduction of transaction costs, lowering the cost of funds, and limitations of managerial ability.

Cooperative Activities in Industrial Groups

Members of industrial groups cooperate with each other in various ways. The most important are cooperative efforts to import energy resources, introduce technology, launch new businesses, and export large turnkey projects.

Major companies in each industrial group are dependent on imported energy resources. (In this sense it is noteworthy that high-technology companies carry comparatively small weight within industrial groups.) Since the markets for raw and processed materials are unstable in both supply and price, and necessitate the distribution of risk, companies dependent on these materials have been forced to seek cooperation with other companies. Furthermore companies dependent on imported energy resources have lacked adequate managerial resources to raise funds and conduct foreign resource developments. To hedge against risks in the markets for raw and processed materials, it is necessary to integrate development, refining, processing, and sales vertically. But few companies dependent on these materials have grown to a size that enables them to undertake such integration. As a result many resource-dependent companies have needed joint ventures.

Cooperation between companies was also necessary for the introduction of technology. Japan's economic growth has been following a technology-borrowing pattern. The introduction of advanced technology from abroad has been one of the important preconditions for companies' success and has required that group member companies cooperate with firms outside their group. In this connection the wide overseas networks of general trading companies have played an important role.

Recently, manufacturing companies have been playing a central role in introducing technology to Japan. Companies importing technology, either by themselves or with other companies, find it difficult to keep track of technological developments worldwide. To overcome such inadequate access to technological information, these companies have increased their cooperation.

Turnkey exports have expanded remarkably since the mid-1970s. Turnkey exports involve the combined export of machinery and materials, and their success depends on cooperation among various companies.

Two points must be made about the relation between turnkey exports and industrial groups. First, mainly involved in turnkey exports are equipment manufacturers, and these are high-technology companies that are usually not highly dependent on the bond of industrial groups but maintain strong, cooperative relations with other companies as far as turnkey exports are concerned. Today's high-technology companies moreover have diversified into the manufacture of many kinds of products, and so they maintain cooperative relationships with industrial groups in transactions involving heavy machinery, a main turnkey export item.

Second, corporations are likely to have cooperative relationships with industrial groups other than their own depending on their export markets. Because the comparative advantage of companies varies by region or country, cooperation with members of its own group or other groups is decided on a case-by-case basis. In recent turnkey exports joint ventures or cooperation with companies of different industrial groups have been increasing, showing further development of independence on the part of companies.

Often member companies cooperate in undertaking new ventures. Industrial groups often jointly participate in undertakings which involve large economies of scale and large capital investments. For example, since the latter half of the 1950s industrial groups have competed with each other to establish new business in the nation's petrochemical industry.

Industrial groups also have been strengthening their cooperation in the aerospace industry, the development of ocean resources, housing construction, and energy development. Cooperation with nonmember companies is likewise increasing, particularly in big projects where future developments are uncertain (see table 8.7).

The Transition of Industrial Groups

The present industrial groups have formed various cooperative relationships that are flexible and economically rational, but due to changes in the business environment the forms of cooperation and competition among members of industrial groups are entering a transitional period. The environmental changes include three conspicuous factors.

First, there is an improvement in individual company financial conditions. Japanese companies needed to strengthen their financial position, and this goal has been nearly attained thanks to Japan's continued high economic growth. The Japanese ratio of net worth to total capital caught up with that of the United States in 1980. As a result

Table 8.7
Six industrial groups' position in Japanese economy

	Net assets	Capital	Current profits	Number of employees
Total for six groups	19.39	19.13	18.51	6.05
Total for three groups of *zaibatsu* origin	9.13	8.44	8.36	2.39
Total for three bank-affiliated groups	10.26	10.68	10.15	3.66
Total for all corporations	100	100	100	100

Note: Actual figures for fiscal 1977, based on the securities reports filed by companies and the Finance Ministry's annual report on corporate statistics. Capital does not include life insurance companies. Current profits do not include property insurance companies. The number of employees does not include those of insurance companies. Figures for companies whose presidents belong to two or more groups are adjusted.

the dependence of companies on industrial groups for funds has been declining.

Second, managerial ability is improving. Japanese business management has had to face one critical situation after another. Now, having accumulated experience and improvement in their financial positions, Japanese managers are able to work out broad and longer-term corporate strategies without outside help. The improvement in managerial ability has been particularly sharp in international transactions. In an increasing number of cases companies are handling their own international operations.

Third, there have been drastic changes in comparative advantage between industries. Although comparative advantage always changes, recent changes in the manufacturing sector have been so great that they have caused conflicts within industrial groups. In the past, shifts in comparative advantage were caused by competition between Japanese companies. Recent shifts, however, have been due to outside factors such as the yen's appreciation in international exchange markets and sharp fluctuations in energy costs.

Companies dependent on raw materials hold the dominant position in industrial groups. Since the supply and price of materials fluctuate sharply, these companies need to cooperate in order to cope with such fluctuations. At present, however, the difference between prices in the Japanese and overseas markets for raw materials for petrochemicals and aluminum is so great that it is impossible for companies in the same industrial group to maintain cooperation.

For example, one textile manufacturer of *zaibatsu* origin was purchasing all of its necessary materials from a chemical company belonging to the same industrial group, not only because the textile manufacturer was a stockholder of the company but also because the chemical firm offered its chemical products at lower prices than did its competitors. However, the yen's appreciation and a rise in materials costs caused a deterioration of the chemical firm's price competitiveness. A rival textile company outside the group began to import lower-priced raw materials, and the textile manufacturer of *zaibatsu* origin requested the chemical company to lower its prices. Because it was impossible to meet the request, the chemical and textile companies belonging to the same industrial group conducted intensive negotiations but failed to reach an agreement. Consequently the textile manufacturer began buying imported chemical products.

The same thing has happened in the case of aluminum. Each industrial group has an aluminum smelting company as a member. But aluminum-consuming companies have been switching to suppliers of lower-priced imported aluminum that are outside their group, causing serious conflicts between aluminum smelters and aluminum-consuming firms within the same industrial group.

New forms of competition have also arisen between member companies in the area of exporting. General trading companies have played a pioneering role in the exports of autos, construction machinery, duplicating machines, and cameras. However, manufacturers have begun to sell their products abroad independently by establishing their own marketing channels. In so doing, they have made efforts to exclude trading companies from their traditional role, despite the existence of interlocking stockholdings between the trading companies and the manufacturers (see table 8.8).

As a result of these environmental changes at home and abroad, competition rather than cooperation is on the rise among member companies of the same industrial group.

Possibility for cooperation depends on whether companies can offer an economic service that promotes cooperation. And recently the frequent occurrence of conflicts between member companies of industrial groups reflects the growing difficulty of offering such a service. Japanese industrial groups are now facing the serious problem of how to coordinate cooperation and competition. For the present they seem to be opting not for cooperation but for competition.

Lester Thurow
Reblending the American Economic Mixture

Competition versus cooperation is not an issue usually raised when Americans start to think about their industrial structure. Because of our history (an isolated continental economic power where large firms exploited their monopoly in the late nineteenth century) and ideology (economies are supposed to be competitive), Americans almost never think about the proper role of cooperation in our industrial structure. Here again a change in the state of the world is going to force changes in American behavior patterns.

Table 8.8
Shift of position in total assets, capital, and sales (percent)

Industrial group	Fiscal 1955	Fiscal 1965	Fiscal 1975	Fiscal 1977
Total for six groups		26.21	24.40	24.79
Total for three groups of *zaibatsu* origin	11.28	12.28	11.93	11.56
Total for three bank-affiliated groups		13.93	12.47	13.23
Total for all corporations	100	100	100	100
Total for six groups		21.15	17.57	18.80
Total for three groups of *zaibatsu* origin	6.91	9.27	8.21	8.13
Total for three bank-affiliated groups		11.88	9.36	10.67
Total for all corporations	100	100	100	100
Total for six groups		13.52	15.18	15.24
Total for three groups of *zaibatsu* origin	5.79	7.07	7.99	7.30
Total for three bank-affiliated groups		6.45	7.20	8.11
Total for all corporations	100	100	100	100

Note: Total assets exclude those of unlisted companies. Capital excludes those of unlisted companies and life insurance companies. Sales exclude those of unlisted companies and financial institutions. Duplication is adjusted. Figures are based on the securities reports filed by companies and the Finance Ministry's annual report on corporate statistics.

The Japanese *zaibatsu*, such as Mitsui, Mitsubishi, Sumitomo, and Yasuda, grew not from strength but from weakness. Cooperation was a vehicle for strengthening weak domestic companies and allowing them to compete against much stronger foreign companies. Information about new technologies and scarce managerial talent were shared; the cost of funds was lower inside a group than outside it; mutual support was forthcoming in bad economic times. The group's trading company would lead a new product into foreign markets and give it aid until the producing company was strong enough and experienced enough to promote the product itself.

In the period when the United States had a huge economic and technological lead over the rest of the world, it was appropriate for American laws to prohibit cooperation among firms. That period is now over. We live in an age of worldwide economic cooperation where a national interpretation of the antitrust laws is out of date. Can it really make sense, for example, that General Motors and Toyota are legally allowed to discuss joint production agreements, whereas under our antitrust laws it is illegal for Ford and General Motors to have such discussions? General Motors could today be the only American car manufacturer, and still it would be in a competitive fight for its life. Although trusts were the major obstacle to competition in the past, today's major obstacle is import restrictions. As long as our borders are open to foreign products, we will live in a competitive economy regardless of the degree of cooperation among American firms.

Cooperation must grow in the United States for the same reason that it grew in Japan: it is needed in a period of economic weakness. This realization is starting to sink in with both governments and firms. A law recently has been passed to make trading companies legal in the United States. Trading companies are not a magic answer, but they are part of the answer. Several groups of firms have recently been given the legal go-ahead to organize cooperative research and development projects. Technological cooperation is not a magic answer, but it is part of the answer. Americans can no longer afford to force five companies to invent the same product independently. It would still be illegal to organize a grouping of firms such as the *zaibatsu,* but perhaps even this is necessary in the present economic weakness.

In the American context almost everyone is hesitant to recommend such changes because of our history. The trusts did abuse their power and attempt to exploit the American consumers. For some reason of social structure or attitude, the Japanese *zaibatsu* did not generate a similar history.

I venture to argue that history could not repeat itself as long as we leave the American market open to foreign competition. More interfirm cooperation will be used not to create irresistible trusts but to prevent American firms from being driven out of markets entirely. What works in economic weakness is not what works in economic strength.

9

Japan's Industrial Policy

Toshimasa Tsuruta

Many overseas observers see cooperative relationships between government and industry as one reason for Japan's economic development. The concept of Japan, Inc., was popularized when James Abegglen in 1970 published his *Study of Japanese Economy—Japan, Inc.* But similar observations had been made in the 1960s. The *London Economist,* for example, had pointed out, though without using the Japan, Inc. concept, that from a Western standpoint Japan's economic system was a kind of planned economy in which industry followed government-drawn grand designs.

It is true that government has played a significant role in Japan's economic development, in both the long process of industrialization after the Meiji restoration in 1868 and in postwar reindustrialization. But the concept of Japan, Inc., is too simplistic to explain the dynamism of the Japanese economy.

The postwar Japanese economy, like those of many Western countries, developed under a market system in which democracy and the price mechanism were main pillars. Japan's postwar economic development began under heavy government protection and assistance. The government adopted protective trade policies and restricted direct foreign investments in Japan to protect its infant industries. It also used fiscal, tax, and monetary measures as part of its strategy. The rapid growth of the Japanese economy in an extremely short period of time attests to the fact that the systems functioned well.

Such government assistance is not peculiar to Japan, as the industrial history of the world shows. Consider such underdeveloped countries in the nineteenth century as France, Germany, and Russia, all of which lagged behind Britain in industrialization during the nineteenth century but later joined the ranks of advanced nations as a result of governments' policies enacted to protect domestic industry. These examples show that it is an established path for developing countries to facilitate industrialization while protecting domestic industry.

Overseas observers of the Japanese economy have often called the Ministry of International Trade and Industry the "notorious MITI" because of its industry-oriented policies. Japan has indeed given the impression of being a nation reluctant to open its markets. Still under import control or subject to high import duties are many products, including oranges, beef, leather, bananas, chocolates, whiskies, cognacs, and marine products—all of which are of prime concern to North American, European, and Southeast Asian countries. It is also true that in Japan, Americans cannot enjoy the same benefits as Japanese enjoy in the United States in services such as data communications, finance, and insurance.

These facts give foreign nations the impression that Japan has a peculiar economic system, but they do not provide evidence that Japan maintains a special economic system. Observing the Japanese economy on the basis of phenomena at a given point in time overlooks the whole process of Japan's gradual removal of government protection and controls. Observing the Japanese economy over a long span of time should provide the understanding that

Japan's postwar economic development has been a process of decontrol and that the protective policies still in place are simply the remains of an economic system established immediately after the war.

Development of Postwar Industrial Policy:
Process of Decontrol

Japan's postwar industrial policy has gone through three stages. The first phase in the 1950s was one of industrial recovery and reconstruction. Two types of policy were implemented to attain that goal. One was the protection of infant industry through import curbs in the form of quotas and restrictions on direct investments. Import quotas were imposed on a broad range of products and by 1955 Japan had liberalized the importation of only 16 percent of such products. Internally direct investments by foreign firms were under control in many key industries with only a few exceptions which were thought to make a great contribution to industrial development.

Industrialization was also promoted through fiscal, tax, and monetary policies. Fiscal policy focused on improving the infrastructure needed for industrialization, whereas tax policy aimed at stepping up capital accumulation and exports through a tax system permitting special depreciation reserves and another exempting a proportion of export earnings. Monetary policy helped the government guide industrialization by channeling funds to strategic industries from the Japan Development Bank and other semiofficial financial institutions.

These policies produced self-supported development of industry and Japan's high economic growth in the second half of the 1950s, the period when the concept of Japan, Inc., fits best. It was then that the government intervened directly in industry by setting import quotas, funneled funds to industry from government-run financial institutions, and granted businesses preferential tax treatment. Clearly government and industry shared a common goal.

But one cannot conclude from such facts that the government-industry cooperative relationship was firmly established, for that is to oversimplify or generalize the question of Japan, Inc. Government and industry were in agreement on the goals of self-reliant industrial development and the strengthening of international competitiveness, but they divided fundamentally, even at this stage, over how to realize those targets.

Government was trying to achieve the goals by restrictive means, whereas industry preferred voluntary action under a market system. This difference over the best means to attain the common targets was a prime reason for sharp government-industry confrontations during the 1960s.

The second phase of industrial policy came in the 1960s. The policy goal during this period was internationalization of the Japanese economy through the liberalization of trade and inward direct investments, in order to adapt it to the international economic order. Policies called for the establishment of a new industrial system and the reorganization of industry. One reason for overseas criticism of MITI as a "notorious" ministry is related to the fact that the government often took a negative attitude toward trade and capital liberalization.

Japan's trade liberalization started in 1960 with government's announcement of an outline of trade and foreign exchange liberalization plans. Liberalization was basically completed in 1963 as far as industrial products were concerned. Further import restrictions were gradually lifted in the 1970s (see table 9.1). Trade liberalization has continued to progress with twenty-seven items left under import control as of January 1982.

The Japanese government's cautious attitude toward trade liberalization can be illustrated by the fact that trade decontrol was carried out step by step and that the government agreed to open the market not willingly but only

Table 9.1
Steps of trade liberalization

| | Number of liberalized items | Items still under importation restriction | | |
		Total	Industrial products	Agricultural products
1962.4	8	466	—	—
10	230	232	—	—
11	8	224	—	—
1963.4	25	197	—	—
6	2	195	—	—
8	35	155	87	68
1964.1	3	152	84	68
2	7	145	77	68
4	8	136	69	67
10	12	123	56	67
1965.10	1	122	55	67
1966.4	2	120	54	66
5	—	126[a]	57	69
10	1	124	56	68
1968.4	2	122	54	68
10	1	121	53	68
1969.4	1	120	52	68
10	2	118	50	68
1970.2	9	109	45	64
4	11	98	39	59
9	8	90	35	55
1971.1	10	80	31	49
6	20	60	20	40
10	20	40	12	28
1972.4	6	33	9	24
1973.4	1	32	8	24
11	1	31	8	23
1974.10	1	30	8	22
12	1	29	7	22
1975.12	2	27	5	22

Source: *Trade Year Book* published by Japan External Trade Association.
a. Increase caused by classification revision of the tariff table.

under pressure from foreign countries. That attitude resulted from the judgment that the main Japanese industries were not competitive enough in international markets. The policy calling for a new industrial system was proposed in order to permit key industries to maintain international competitiveness during a period of trade liberalization. It translated into a bill proposed in 1963 to vitalize specific industries.

The government advanced two proposals. One called for the establishment of a government-industry cooperative system aimed at renovating the mutual relationship. The other envisaged the promotion of oligopoly through industrial concentration and merger. Behind the proposals was concern over market structure and intense industrial competition. The government knew that many companies in key industries were small in size when considered in the international context. It was also concerned over what it referred to as excessive competition in the business community. This was illustrated by a series of new entries into various sectors of industry and keen competition in undercutting prices. The charge of excessive competition was also explained by lending competition among city banks and major commercial banks with nationwide service networks.

The proposed system of government-industry cooperation sought to replace the free play of market forces, such as the price mechanism, with artificial adjustments by setting up a forum for consultations among industrial, financial, academic, and government representatives in order to establish a cooperative system so that industries could strengthen their international position. The policy of promoting oligopoly was designed to overcome the internationally small scale of business, regarded as a weak point common to principal industries.

Japan, Inc., would have come into being if these policies had been realized. They probably also would have curtailed the vitality of the Japanese economy, and it is doubtful that Japan would have successfully ridden out the oil crisis. Fortunately the proposed legislation was abandoned in 1964 after parliamentary debate.

There were two causes of its failure. One was the ruling Liberal-Democratic party's negative stance toward the law, stemming from objections by industry which feared government control. The other was objections from the opposition camp such as the Japan Socialist party and the Democratic Socialist party, which claimed that the legislation was questionable in the light of the antimonopoly law.

A similar government proposal for industrial reorganization was made in connection with the liberalization of capital in the late 1960s. A theory favoring economies of scale swept through Japan as capital liberalization became necessary after Japan joined the OECD in 1964. According to this view, capital liberalization required stepped-up consolidation of Japanese businesses through mergers in order to compete with the American and European corporate giants.

The policy of facilitating mergers was based on the belief that labor control, fund raising, technological development, marketing, and administrative management were all in proportion to corporate size. It was believed that the larger a business the better its business capabilities. Another factor behind the government's promotion of industrial reshaping was the merger movement between major companies then taking place in Western Europe. It constituted an important element that helped create the myth of economies of scale in Japan.

The government's policy of capital liberalization was implemented step by step in and after 1967; 100 percent decontrol was basically achieved in 1973. The industrial reorganization promoted during this period did not, however, proceed according to the government's scenario, as was the case with the establishment of a new industrial system through government-industry cooperation. For example, the merger of Yawata and Fuji steel mills into Nippon Steel Corp. symbolized the government policy of industrial reorganization, but the antimonopoly law deadlocked that particular merger. Not until the two firms accepted Fair Trade Commission (FTC) recommendations based on the law could they finally merge. After announcement of the merger plan, it took one and a half years for the companies and the FTC to hammer out a mutually satisfactory ruling on the case. The government also tried but failed to have three major paper mills—Oji, Jujo, and Honshu—merge back into a single company, as they had been before the war.

It is worth noting that, against the background of internationalization, corporate policy choices went beyond the scope of government industrial policy. An example was the capital linkup between Mitsubishi Motors and Chrysler announced in 1969. One of government's main goals in industrial policy was to protect domestic business; such a viewpoint was an essential element in carrying out industrial reshaping in connection with capital decontrol. The strategic automobile industry in particular was a sector that MITI wanted to protect from foreign control. In Japan-U.S. talks in 1968 over the liberalizations of investments in the automobile industry, MITI came up with two principles: not to specify the date of capital liberalization for the industry and not to permit partnership between existing Japanese automakers and foreign competitors. Mitsubishi Motors's choice clearly violated the government's industrial policy framework. MITI wanted to liberalize capital investments in the automobile industry after consolidating smaller automakers into a third group next to Toyota and Nissan through merger and other means. The Mitsubishi-Chrysler linkup appeared to be a "totally regrettable development" to MITI.

The third stage of industrial policy occurred in the 1970s, when the Japanese economy was hit by the "Nixon shock" (the upward revaluation of the yen in 1971), the oil crisis, and high inflation during 1972–74. The conditions that had permitted rapid postwar economic growth changed dramatically. As a result the growth rate of the Japanese economy slowed considerably. The necessary industrial adjustments strained trade relations with foreign countries. The climate of industrialization also changed, from one ignoring the environment to giving preference to it over industrial development. This change followed the conclusion of four major lawsuits on pollution from 1971 to 1973. In addition the antimonopoly law was revised in 1977 for the first time since the end of the war. Controls on unfair trade practices were tightened, giving competition a central role in industrial policy.

In the 1970s industrial policy sought to establish restrictive policies based on new rules, such as the tougher antimonopoly law, and laid greater emphasis on environmental protection. Industrial adjustments were made in connection with trade conflicts and in response to domestic pressures.

In summary, the theme of Japan's industrial policy has shifted every ten years: from the protection of infant industries and the promotion of industrialization at an early stage, to internationalization and the establishment of a new industrial system at the intermediate stage, and then to the introduction of restrictive policies based on new rules and industrial adjustments. Such changes have mirrored the postwar development of the Japanese economy and the alterations in basic economic conditions.

The changes also suggest that except for the immediate postwar policy, industrial policy did not proceed by discerning specific problems, working to solve them, and carrying out policies with specific objectives. Rather, trade and capital liberalization, for example, were developed in response to foreign pressure.

The yen's upward revaluation in 1971 was also sparked by foreign pressure. Behind the policy switch to environmental protection and tighter control under the strengthened antimonopoly law was domestic pressure: the four antipollution trials and growing public criticism of a rush of cartel arrangements immediately after the first oil crisis. Japan's industrial policy was not built firmly, as suggested by the Japan, Inc., hypothesis, nor did it work actively on Japan's industrial society from a long-term perspective. In reality it evolved in an impromptu fashion in order to cope, hastily, with individual issues.

Price Mechanism versus Industrial Policy: Policy Failure in the Auto Industry

To understand Japan's industrial policy, two different aspects must be considered. One is that various policies designed to help industry adopted at an early stage of Japan's economic development indirectly guided industrialization through the aid of the price mechanism. Every means available—fiscal, tax, and monetary policies—were taken to help such indirect guidance. That aspect of industrial policy contributed to sustained fast economic growth and the stronger international competitiveness of industry starting in the second half of the 1950s.

The other face of the postwar policy had a negative effect; it distorted industrial performance. The government tried to intervene through restrictive means in pricing, output, capital spending, and other private variables that should be determined according to the economic cycle. Another example is the adoption of an oligopolistic policy designed to promote mergers.

The two policy stances are not compatible. A stronger government intervention would have choked the price mechanism, making it almost impossible to maintain the growth of the Japanese economy. It is safe to say the rapid shift in industrial structure under Japan's fast postwar economic growth was based fundamentally on the function of the price mechanism. The nation's industry became so competitive internationally as to cause trade friction with many other countries. Under the force of the price mechanism, many businesses were highly innovative.

But it is true that the government pushed intervention in industrial activity and the creation of oligopolistic businesses. Here lies the factual basis on which rests the idea of Japan, Inc., pointing to government-industry cooperation.

How could Japan maintain a favorable economic performance generally, despite frequent government intervention restricting competition? That question seems to be a key to understanding Japan's industrial policy.

The answer is that there were moves within the economy itself to promote competition helping the free play of market forces to break through the framework of government intervention. The Japanese economy was able to perform so well because government intervention limiting competition was focused mainly on basic industries producing key industrial materials such as steel. Little direct intervention occurred in processing-type industries directly linked to market demand, though there was intervention through indirect government guidance.

The processing industries faced radical structural changes due to rapid growth. These structural changes in turn permitted the basic industries to focus their full attention on economies of scale. The quest of such economic rationalism eventually allowed the barrier of government intervention to be broken.

A typical example of unsuccessful government intervention in the processing industries can be seen in the automobile industry—the most important industry developed in the postwar process of industrialization. Automobile production induced new output in a host of fringe industries and offered many new job opportunities. For that reason the government decided to protect the automobile industry in 1952, curbing imports under a quota system. Import controls continued until October 1965, helping the industry to become well established.

The government tried to develop the automobile industry under the framework of a protective policy. In May 1955 MITI announced a draft outline of a program to develop a national car. The plan called for fostering a minicar as a new industry in a bid to expand related industries, increase employment, improve technical levels, and lay the groundwork for the future development of an automobile export industry. The plan sought to have a single company mass-produce an ultra-small popular car that was inexpensive and exportable. MITI granted manufacturers of such cars official financial aid and legal protection with a view to establishing car production as an independent industry. The plan failed because it was based on too much government control.

MITI's national car plan was unreasonable from the start in that it sought to put it into force within the framework of market economy. When MITI announced the plan in 1955, just a decade after the end of the war, the framework of government control that continued into the immediate postwar years from prewar days had already been scrapped and a market-economy system had taken root in Japan. The Japanese economy had entered a period when consumer choices significantly affected corporate performance. It had become impossible for companies to grow without taking the market into account.

In fact Toyota Motors was trying to set up its own Toyota production system eclipsing a Ford system in a move to stand on its feet based on its own technology. Other major companies were beginning to pursue growth through technical linkups with overseas firms; such agreements in 1952 included those between Nissan Motors and Austin of Britain, Isuzu Motors and Rootes Motors also of Britain, and Hino Motors and Renault of France. The MITI plan was unacceptable to those automakers seeking to establish their own growth strategies.

The pursuit of their own techniques based on partnership with foreign manufacturers led Japan's automobile industry to follow a growth pattern in the late 1950s and 1960s totally different from what MITI had envisaged in its national car plan. Instead, competition developed among companies—competition that helped improve product quality, cut prices, and diversify car models. Japanese automakers rushed to build car plants seeking to establish a mass-production setup in preparation for trade liberalization in the 1960s.

Simultaneously, MITI was calling for the consolidation of automakers into a smaller number of firms. Announced in June 1961 by a subcommittee of an advisory panel to MITI, the MITI plan sought to reorganize the industry into three groups, each comprising two or three automakers. One group was to consist of mass-producers, targeting output at 10,000 units a month in 1965, with each firm producing one model. The second group would comprise manufacturers of specialty cars such as sports and quality cars, and the third group, makers of minicars. The consolidation plan was designed to hold down new entry into the car market and thus generate the same effect of mass production as under the national car plan.

When MITI announced its consolidation plan, competition was beginning to intensify in the automobile industry between different models and between companies. In the late 1960s Honda Motors, a motorcycle producer, entered the car market. The series of new entries to the market was based on the expectation that Japan's car market would rapidly grow and that consumer demand would lead to growing market opportunities for new or different models. To cope with the second situation, leading automakers such as Toyota and Nissan came out with new models in an effort to offer a full line of cars.

Today there are nine car manufacturers in Japan. No other industrial country has so many automakers. Clearly this growth resulted from a development path quite different from MITI's plan of an automobile industry consisting of a small number of manufacturers. MITI maintained its idea until a capital agreement was announced by Mitsubishi and Chrysler in 1969. Not until then did MITI realize the unrealistic nature of its policy for the industry.

MITI's failure to intervene in the automobile industry offers two lessons. One is how it is important for an industry to go through the tests of the market for its development. The other is that there are limitations to government intervention. MITI lacked the legal power to curb new entries or influence output, prices, and capital spending. The second point shows that administrative guidance practiced in Japan has limitations.

What Ensures Policy Effectiveness?

Government intervention consists roughly of intervention based on laws and intervention without legal endorsement—administrative guidance. In evaluating Japan's industrial policy it is important to observe how much intervention is conducted on the basis of legal support. It is essentially impossible to put into practice any government-drafted grand policy design unless the government intervention is backed by legally binding authority.

Advocates of the Japan, Inc., hypothesis are inclined to think the government is deeply committed to the activity of many industries. But there are not many examples of institutional intervention in the case of the manufacturing industry, which constitutes the main pillar of the Japanese economy—although direct intervention in output, prices, and capital investments is observed in agriculture, transportation, communication, and finance. To put it more precisely, the legal or other support necessary to ensure the effectiveness of government intervention has been lost since trade and capital were liberalized.

There are two types of institutional intervention having binding power: intervention based on general laws and on specific legislation. The former type of intervention that affected industrial activity included intervention through the allocation of import quotas, which was carried out until trade liberalization occurred in the 1960s, and through the exercise of authority, based on the foreign investment law, to permit new entry and capital investments, which was conducted until capital liberalization. The latter type of intervention was limited to only a few industries dependent totally on foreign technology, such as petrochemicals.

Of vital importance to the development of postwar industrial policy were the mandates for import quotas, new entry, and capital spending. Because the government was legally able to step into industry, government-led industrialization was realized, as in the case of the petrochemical industry. Trade and capital liberalization has meant the loss of legally binding power that once ensured the effectiveness of government intervention. That viewpoint is important in a consideration of industrial policy.

When the government tried to enact a new law for invigorating specific industries in connection with trade liberalization, it set up a framework for developing an industry policy through new legislation, and it tried to alter the government-industry relationship through the policy of industrial reorganization. All of the policies represented stopgap efforts to compensate for the lack of an established policy when trade and capital decontrol occurred in the 1960s. One can conclude that trade and capital liberalization in the 1960s led to a complete collapse of the government policy known as Japan, Inc.

Not all government intervention based on general laws has ended. Four pieces of legislation leave the door open to government intervention: (1) export and import trade control orders and the export/import trading law, both permitting government formation of export and import cartels; (2) a law authorizing the establishment of organizations of small- and medium-sized firms, which allows government intervention in the creation of cartels by smaller businesses; (3) an emergency law designed to *stabilize national economic life*, enacted during the first oil crisis; and (4) a temporary law calling for the stabilization of specific troubled industries and some other laws that permit government interference in the price of general goods and services in structurally depressed industries, which require concerted action in scrapping surplus equipment. A fifth should probably be added: as an exception to antimonopoly law rules, it is possible to make antirecession cartel arrangements for joint production cutbacks.

These systems cannot necessarily be justified in the light of policy favoring competition, but it cannot be supposed that the presence of these laws leads to constant government intervention. Case 1, for example, is the remains of import restrictions in the 1950s, and today's application of the trade control orders is limited to export curbs in times of trade friction (such as voluntary restraints on car exports begun in 1981).

The law in case 2 was legislated in the 1950s to help modernize smaller businesses. There are examples of cost-cutting cartels in the 1950s and 1960s in some industries, but these artificial adjustments did not always succeed. The law no longer has any real meaning today. An example of the law's broad application is in the textile industry where the law helps control capital investments by smaller businesses in the midstream to downstream areas of the industry. But this government intervention is in line with a series of curbs on textile exports under a Japan-U.S. cotton textile trade agreement concluded in 1957. Artificial adjustments boost costs and are not necessarily desirable for the Japanese economy. Case 3 is applied in emergencies such as OPEC's cut in crude oil supplies in 1973 and has no significance in a normal state of affairs.

Thus government intervention based on general legislation does not necessarily have substantial meaning in evaluating today's economic performance. Because economic adjustments in the wake of the oil crisis were left to the market mechanisms and not to government, the Japanese economy could maintain its favorable performance after the oil crunch. If the government had displaced powerful leadership, as the Japan, Inc., hypothesis assumes, the process of economic adjustments would have gone through rough sailing. The case of the oil-refining industry is pertinent in this regard, for it is a typical example of industrial organization distorted by deep government involvement in industrialization.

Examples of government intervention based on specific laws were often observed in the course of the promotion of industrialization. They were based on laws of limited duration designed to revitalize particular industries. But it was only in the early stage of industrialization, the 1950s, that these laws were of great significance. Most of the laws were designed to open the way for lending by the government-financed Japan Development Bank, as well as to give the industries involved their rationalization targets. They helped to supplement the market mechanisms.

The 1962 oil business law was of a totally different nature. The oil business law was enacted to prevent the entry of foreign oil firms in the wake of decontrol on crude oil imports carried out as part of trade liberalization in the 1960s. It was also designed to nurture and aid domestic oil companies. It authorized MITI's restrictive intervention in a broad range of corporate operations. The law required any company to seek MITI approval when entering the oil-refining industry or installing new or additional equipment. It also obliged companies to submit plans on the output of petroleum products and crude oil imports. The law further authorized MITI to recommend revision of output according to changes in supply and demand and to set standard prices on oil products.

Such issues as when to install new or extra equipment, at what level to maintain output, and what prices to set are the most important concepts of private enterprise. They are determined independently by companies on the basis of their short- and long-term management strategies. In the oil-refining industry, however, decision making on these matters was affected by MITI's control.

The passage of the oil business law in 1962 resulted in great distortions in the industry's structure. Once the law was enacted, the government committed itself to the industry's formation against the background of comprehensive authority. In particular, the government tried to develop Japanese-owned oil firms by exercising its right to permit new entries and expansion of equipment. As a result of such industrial management (or administrative guidance), the industry swarmed with a host of competitors, thirty-four distributors and refiners had come into being as of 1981. Today the oil-refining industry faces a number of structural problems: the presence of small refiners, a gap between refining and marketing capabilities, a distorted pricing system for oil products, a gap in its ability to procure crude oil, and the loss of corporate vitality.

The gap between refining and marketing capacity resulted, evidently, from MITI's administrative guidance designed to develop domestically owned oil firms. With MITI-led supply-demand adjustments for oil products always creating a gap not only in the general supply-demand relationship but between corporate supply and demand, the refining-marketing gap sharpened price fluctuations, hampering normal development of the industry. The industry has long sought to eliminate that gap.

Excessive price fluctuations helped strengthen administrative intervention in output allocation and price formation. The oil-refining industry's violation of the antimonopoly law was what MITI's administrative guidance brought forth. The industry has been hit hard by steep rises in crude oil prices since the oil crisis, and the question of its reorganization is inevitable. Because the industry's structure was formed by administrative intervention, it has lost its ability to adapt to economic realities.

There are two options for coping. One is industrial reorganization led by administrative guidance as in the past;

the other is to leave it for automatic adjustment by the price mechanism. For the present the government is following the former course, but that choice does not necessarily guarantee success in view of past government intervention. The government seems unable to face the limitations of Japan, Inc.

Shift in Antimonopoly Policy and Process
of Tightened Application

Supporters of the Japan, Inc., hypothesis are likely to overlook the fact that there is an antimonopoly law in force in Japan. True, the history of the law is shorter than that of the U.S. antitrust act, which was introduced in Japan in 1947 as part of occupation policy. And it can hardly be denied that the law is not as ingrained as in the United States. Nevertheless, the law has functioned effectively and has contributed to creating today's competitive order in the Japanese economy.

Over the years Japan's antimonopoly policy has been gradually strengthened. Attempts to solidify the antimonopoly policy and have it take root in Japan's industrial society have always been stronger than attempts to overturn the antimonopoly law. The process can be divided, as was the case with the development of industrial policy, into three phases, 1950s, 1960s, and 1970s and later.

Antimonopoly policy was in retreat in the 1950s, symbolized by the 1953 revision of the antimonopoly law. Carried out under a request from industry, the revision eased restrictions on cartels and trusts. For example, the cartel restrictions were relaxed to permit a resale price system (designed to maintain retail prices at given levels), anti-recession cartels, and rationalization cartels as exceptions to a general rule banning cartels. The trust curbs were eased on corporate stock ownership and the holding of concurrent posts by board members. The 1953 revision also expanded systems restricting competition. An example is the enforcement of competition-curbing measures by government agencies such as production cutbacks designed to cope with recessions (such cutback orders were terminated around 1965). Such recommendations established limits to the FTC's application of the antimonopoly law. Another instance is an expansion in 1953 of laws excluding from the antimonopoly law smaller-business associations and the export-import trading law, both enacted in 1952. Mergers among trading companies and financial institutions originating from the prewar *zaibatsu* or financial combines were carried out under the eased trust restrictions. Thus the antimonopoly law during this period was inactive under the pressure of government policies for promoting industrialization.

Antimonopoly policy in the 1960s can be placed in a continuous flow of an industry-first policy stance. Nevertheless, the decade was a period when a shift in antimonopoly policy was burgeoning. The Japanese economy faced trade and capital liberalization. With Japan's switching to an open economy, industrial policy was focused on the establishment of an industrial system that could cope with the liberalization. A bill for revitalizing specific industries was proposed by the government in an effort to set up such a system. The proposed legislation went nowhere due to objections from industries that opposed government control. The government then tried to set up a system of government-industry cooperation. Industry called for a system of voluntary adjustments—in effect an industrial system without government intervention.

Both MITI and industry saw the need to streamline the industrial system to cope with trade liberalization, but they could not agree how to do it. There was a theme common to both: further weakening of the antimonopoly law. MITI intended to do so by new legislation, which would exempt from the law corporate amalgamations that would in effect restrict competition. Industry called for revision of the law and proposed the following: easing of requirements for arranging cartels, tolerating concerted action to avoid excessive competition, sharply expanding rationalization cartels, permitting cartels to step up exports, greatly easing restrictions on merger, and relaxing provisions on holding companies. Had these proposals been enacted into law, the antimonopoly law would have been killed. Industry's objection to the law was deeply rooted. In 1958 a bill revising the law, incorporating all these proposals was submitted to the Diet, but it was eventually scrapped.

Fortunately for the Japanese economy, neither the proposed legislation for revitalizing specific industries nor the second revision of the antimonopoly law materialized. If the legislation had been approved, Japan, Inc., would certainly have come into existence. And it seems that if the revision had been realized, many trusts would have appeared, bringing about a rigid economic structure. The basic reason that these provisions never came about is that the development of postwar democracy brought with it public objections to monopoly.

A battle over MITI's industry-reshaping policy was fought out in connection with the merger between Yawata and Fuji steel companies into Nippon Steel. Judging from the outcome, many people believe that the merger, creating the world's largest steelmaker, was a defeat for antimonopoly policy, but a closer look at the merger process shows a shift in antimonopoly policy.

First, the FTC approved the merger in the form of a ruling that was worked out through a series of legal procedures involving preliminary investigation, formal screening and a trial. It took one and a half years to reach the ruling after the merger plan was announced. This was the first time since passage of the antimonopoly law that a merger plan was disputed and subjected to an FTC trial.

Second, the merger was approved only after the two companies accepted FTC recommendations calling on them to divest themselves of operations involving railing, tinplate, sheet piling, and pig iron for cast products. It is still disputed in Japan today whether such a ruling was reasonable, but it is certain that the merger did not take place without acceptance of the FTC recommendations. The ruling is worth attention as one indicating the FTC's policy stance toward merger, which forced the MITI-led policy of industrial reorganization to collapse.

Third, the antimonopoly law gained public support in the 1960s for the first time in its twenty-year history. This is indicated by a chorus of objections to the merger from economists, consumer groups, and other private interests who aroused public opinion in opposition to the government, the ruling Liberal-Democratic party, and the business community. Statements and articles by economists and experts carried in various magazines contributed to the public debates. Newspapers reported developments on both sides in detail. It was the first time in Japan that most sectors of journalism took up a single economic topic— merger of two steel companies—which also was a sophisticated legal case involving the antimonopoly law.

The third stage of antimonopoly policy came in the 1970s as the antimonopoly law was gradually strengthened. The question of market control by oligopolistic companies was already spotlighted through such incidents as unauthorized setting of resale prices by Matsushita Electric Industrial Co. and Sony Corp., the Yawata-Fuji merger (both in 1967) and dual pricing for television sets in 1971. These incidents laid the groundwork for reinforcing the antimonopoly law. A decisive development that prompted revision of the law in favor of tougher control on monopoly was a series of unauthorized cartel arrangements made in many industries amid galloping inflation immediately after the oil crisis.

Behind the rush of illegal cartels was a sellers' market accompanied by high inflation which produced an economic climate where it was easy to form cartels. Another factor was the absence of antimonopoly law clauses setting forth punitive measures against illegal cartels. To cope with that absence, a bill strengthening the law was introduced to the Diet in 1975 and again in 1977. It incorporated new measures such as imposition of surcharges, the sale of part of operations, and tighter control on corporate stock holdings. The bill passed the Diet under the Fukuda administration.

In evaluating Japan's competition policy since the revision of the antimonopoly law, two other points are worth noting. One is that in the 1980 ruling on an unauthorized cartel by the oil industry criminal penalties were levied for the first time on a price-fixing cartel. MITI's administrative guidance in the oil business law was also found to be in violation of the antimonopoly law. The other point is that the FTC's antimonopoly administration was expanded to cover distribution as well as manufacturing, its original target. This is illustrated by the FTC's policy announced in 1980 to tighten restrictions on moves by oligopolistic manufacturers to affiliate distributors with their groups. The FTC, along with such curbs on distribution, is also tightening control over the growing power of major retailers enjoying oligopolistic positions in some parts of the country.

In sum, the postwar history of antimonopoly administration can be regarded as a process in which the antimonopoly law acquired respectability. It was a process in which the importance of traditional industrial policy faded away.

Industrial Adjustments since the Oil Crisis and Policy Stance

The stance of traditional industrial policy changed radically around 1970. A May 1971 report from MITI's advisory panel, the Industrial Structure Council, says that "the sense of concentrating on the one point of solely seeking larger-scale operations is a remnant of a past age" and adds that "the time is over for believing that one has only to be intent on strengthening international competitiveness." Such a shift in policy stance mirrored changes of the times.

In 1968 the Japanese economy, as measured by GNP, became the second largest in the noncommunist world after the United States, and Japan's balance of payments swung from deficit to surplus on current account around 1967. These developments required Japan to change its policy stance from one of a small country to an economic power. Another factor behind the policy switch was the development of urban congestion and rural decline, increasingly serious environmental pollution by industry, and monopolistic market control by oligopolistic businesses.

As a new version of its industrial policy, MITI came up with a plan to develop knowledge-intensive industries. The plan sought to place high-value-added, highly processing industries at the heart of Japan's industrial structure. The industrial structure has already changed in the wake of the oil crisis with knowledge-intensive industries assuming a central role. But the change resulted not from MITI's industrial policy but rather from the function of the market mechanism. The two oil crises merely accelerated the shift.

MITI's knowledge-intensive plan was a novel proposal at the time. Announced in May 1971, or just before the oil crisis, the plan was impossible to pursue with a clear sense of objectives as an industrial policy in the 1970s except for the development of very large-scale integration (VLSI) chips and some other projects. This was because the MITI plan was followed by a series of economic upheavals. Under such conditions the government had to adapt industrial policy to cope with the problems. Such ex-post-facto adaptation of industrial policy was directed to adjustments of domestic industry and trade friction. Industrial policy cushioned the impact of the market mechanism.

Rises in oil prices in the wake of the oil crisis made adjustment of the industrial structure inevitable. The following two positions indicate what policy stance the government should take concerning industrial adjustments. One is government-led adjustments through intervention. The other is to entrust industrial adjustments basically to market mechanisms, limiting government intervention to employment problems produced by such adjustments.

It is almost impossible for the government to step into each process of adjustment as long as higher oil prices affect the supply structure in various sectors of industry. Such adjustments result from individual corporate choices through which companies adapt to changes in markets. It is a process of technical progress involving changes in the combination of production elements. In that process are most effectively displayed the originality and innovation of each company.

In Japan competition is intense between companies and between products. In such an economy it is almost impossible to pass on cost increases to consumers in the form of higher prices. Instead, companies must maximize productivity gains in order to absorb cost increases. Technical progress ensures corporate existence and growth in a competitive economy. Moves toward technical progress are particularly noticeable in the processing industries near to final market demand, resulting in remarkable gaps in wholesale price rises according to the use of products as shown in figure 9.1. The price rises on capital and durble consumer goods were very stable during the oil crisis.

Industrial adjustments induced by the oil crisis were carried out generally under the force of market mechanisms. Such shifts in the industrial structure were not conducted smoothly, however. As a result of entrusting industrial adjustments to market mechanisms, Japan now faces the question of unbalanced development between processing and basic industries. As a result of the oil crisis some basic industries have lost their international competitive edge, leaving their adjustment a major task for the 1980s.

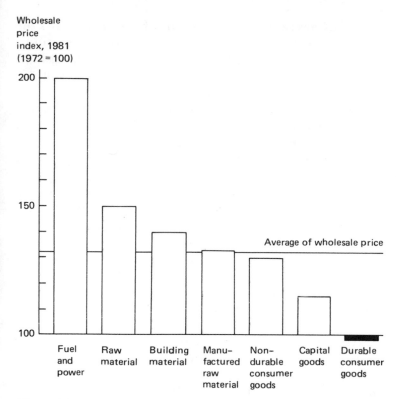

Figure 9.1
Price rises according to the use of products (1975–1980).

Since the oil crisis the unbalanced development of processing and basic industries has become a major issue. For example, the index of production for the processing industry stood at about 200 in 1981 against the 1975 average of 100, while it was only 110 in the case of the basic industry. The former industries were able to grow quickly through export expansion, but the latter was shut. The growth of the Japanese economy slowed while technical progress in the processing industry resulted in a sharp decline in the ratio of intermediate input from basic industries, thereby reducing the growth of the market for the latter industry. And basic industries lost international competitiveness, facing withdrawal from the export market and fiercer competition with imports. The result was sagging plant operations and profit ratios.

The government's policy stance since the oil crisis has been to leave industrial adjustments in the hands of market forces with the government giving preference to employment adjustments. Such behavior can be termed prudent. But the government did not have a nonintervention policy for all industries. In 1978 it enacted a special law, to be in effect for five years, to bail out industries caught in a protracted slump due to factors caused by the oil crisis. The temporary law designed to stabilize specific recession-hit industries opened the way for the disposal of surplus capacity. Among industries covered by the law were steelmaking, aluminum smelting, synthetic textiles, linear board and corrugated cardboard, fertilizer, and shipbuilding. At the same time the FTC permitted some industries, mainly those producing basic materials, to form antirecession cartels as an emergency measure.

There are various interpretations of such government intervention, but probably all will agree that these government moves were nothing more than measures aimed at easing a supply resulting from the oil crisis; they were passive responses.

In other words, it is important that market forces worked so strongly in the course of adjustments since the oil crisis that the government had no choice but to react passively. But such government reactions have their limitations. There are limitations to resuscitating industries whose international position has been weakened by the supply shock of the oil crisis. Among basic industries that face adjustments of this sort are those using oil as a main raw material such as petrochemical, oil refining, vinyl chloride, and fertilizer, and those using oil in the form of electricity, such as aluminum smelting, zinc, and other nonferrous metals. The industries in the first group have lost advantages due to competition from North America firms using low-cost natural gas. Those in the second group have been hit by Japan's high cost of electricity.

The industrial adjustments that surfaced in basic industry means a collapse of the all-inclusive industrial structure built up since the war. This is unavoidable given today's progress in the international division of labor and internationalization of the domestic market. It is basically impossible today for Japan to try to protect industry. For example, the aluminum smelting industry was capable of producing 1.6 million tons of ingot during the high-growth period. That capacity fell to 1.1 million tons in 1980 as the industry disposed of surplus equipment in the wake of an import surge. The second oil crisis worsened the industry's relative disadvantage, inviting a phenomenal rise in ingot imports. To cope with it, the Aluminum Division of MITI's Industrial Structure Council recommended in October 1981 that the industry maintain smelting capacity of 700,000 tons, with fiscal 1985, ending on March 31, 1986, as a target year. But the actual pace of adjustment was faster than under the MITI plan; with major aluminum smelters deciding in 1982–83 to withdraw partially or totally from domestic smelting, capacity has shrunk to about 300,000 tons.

MITI plans to maintain domestic production in basic industry for economic security reasons and is discussing ways to do so, but it has become impossible to put any such plans into force. Japan was able to build an all-around industrial structure in the postwar years because of five factors:

1. Japan was allowed to impose import restrictions to protect its infant industry.

2. There was a climate at home permitting the use of fiscal, monetary, and other policies to promote industrial development.

3. Cheap crude oil, $1 per barrel, was available without limit in supply.

4. A fixed exchange rate of 360 yen to the U.S. dollar was maintained, permitting a continuous shift to export industries unlike the current system of floating exchange rates.

5. Japan had only to consider catching up with U.S. and European nations in the absence of competition such as is now emerging from the newly industrialized countries.

Today conditions surrounding Japan have changed completely. Even if a plan is prepared showing what this or that should look like, only the market knows if it is possible to realize the plan. Thus one can conclude that Japan no longer can have an adjustment system that will replace or supplement market forces.

This means a collapse of the mythical Japan, Inc., hypothesis. Like many other industrial countries, Japan is facing the difficulties of a mature economy. Industrial policy cannot reverse the flow of history. This is the most important point in understanding the Japanese economy.

Lester Thurow
Reblending the American Economic Mixture

Planning versus the price mechanism is a traditional American dichotomy, yet one the Japanese illustrate need not exist. Industrial policies are used to restructure old industries to make the market viable and to push new industries so that they will expand faster. The aim of industrial policies is to link the virtues of planning with the virtues of the market, not to use one to thwart the other.

As is illustrated in the automobile case, industrial policies are also not carried out by top-down central planning where private firms take orders from government agencies. Firms can resist industrial policies. Automakers were successful despite industrial policies and did not receive the government aid that goes with those policies. At the same time other industries have become successful with the aid of industrial policies. But to think of planning as a synonym for centralization is mistaken. The goal is decentralization while maintaining the virtues of coordination and strategic planning where they are useful.

To be successful, industrial policies have to be applied with discretion. Yet the American tradition is one of giving government officials little discretion. They are boxed in with rules and regulations to ensure that they are fair and do not abuse their power. Perhaps this history could be overcome if industrial policies were deliberately linked with the investment banking issue.

Large investment banks, whether public or private, must have a strategic view of where the country should be going when they make their lending decisions. In their investment decisions they will create an implicit industrial policy even if they do not explicitly recognize the function. As a result, if we were to recreate both public and private investment banking at the same time, we would be automatically introducing a strong element of industrial policy-making into our economy without at the same time either centralizing it or increasing government involvement. Discretion could be introduced into public investment banking decisions because at the same time we would be introducing a new aspect of discretionary decision making in the private economy. The two sets of investment banks could cooperate where that seemed wise and go their separate ways where that seemed wise.

The market mechanism can also be linked with planning through the requirement that both sides approve of a project before it is undertaken. Thus the fifth-generation computer project is 50 percent financed by MITI, but the other 50 percent must come from the private sector. If the private sector is unwilling to finance its share, the project is not undertaken, no matter how good it looks to govern-

ment officials. By contrast, in the supersonic transport case
the Boeing Corporation wanted government to take all of
the risks in building the plane. As has since been shown in
the case of the European SST, to do so would have been a
mistake. At the same time there are valid reasons for
spreading the risk of large, prospectively viable projects
across society. What is a project with little risk to a country is
often a tremendous risk for one company.

Perhaps more important than any specific success or
failure of industrial policies is the effect that they can have
on attitudes and social consensus. Countries are ultimately
groups of people who share the same strategic vision. I am
impressed when I visit Japan to be widely told that Japan's
economic strategy is to get out of energy-based industries
and into knowledge-based industries and to have the
world's highest per-capita GNP by the year 2000. A shared
strategic economic vision is one of those ties that binds and
helps each individual relate his or her small task to the
bigger vision.

10

Economic Planning in Japan

Saburo Okita

The Experience of Economic Planning in Japan

Although the Japanese government has produced several economic plans since the end of World War II and has an economic planning agency, the Japanese economy is not a planned economy. It is a predominantly private-enterprise economy. Occasionally government intervenes in private activities, but the basic nature of the present Japanese economy is a highly competitive market economy.

Contrary to the prevailing image, Japan today is characterized by keen competition among enterprises, big and small. The market share of companies in various branches of industry is still fluid, and a number of firms have been established since World War II, such as Sony and Matsushita. The private sector is very dynamic, and it maintains the flexibility of a competitive market system to a large degree.

There are, however, two conflicting trends in government-business relations. One is the historical role of the government. Nearly a century ago Japan, an economically underdeveloped and industrially backward country, began to modernize. The government strongly backed the modernization and gave protection, encouragement, and inducement to new industries. This paternalistic attitude of the government toward private industry has been diminishing gradually as a result of the rapid expansion and strengthening of private industry. Direct intervention by the government in individual private enterprises is practiced to a very small extent in present-day Japan.

On the other hand, there are increasing government responsibilities for preventing unemployment and serious business fluctuations, for improving social overhead capital, for expanding educational and training facilities, for maintaining fair competition, for promoting social security, and for preventing pollution.

In Japan economic planners have avoided introducing strong planning elements into the private sector and have stated explicitly in their plans that the figures for the private sector are only estimates and that the responsibility for making plans and implementing them rests with the private enterprises themselves. Government plans provide only guidelines for the decisions to be made by private enterprises and the broad outlines of the government policies that will influence industry.

In Japan, however, there is general recognition of the usefulness of planning in a free-enterprise economy. And the preparation of the economic plans has had an educational effect on the various ministries, on business, on labor unions, and on the general public.

Government planners have also been embarrassed by the unpredictability of economic growth. When the 1958–1962 plan was being prepared in 1957, nobody predicted a 13 percent annual growth of GNP in real terms—an average that actually was reached during 1959, 1960, and 1961. When the National Income Doubling Plan of 1961–1970 was being processed in early 1960, no economist expected the ratio of gross capital formation to GNP to rise from the level of 30 percent (actual data for 1956–1958) to the much higher level of 37 percent reached in 1961–1963. Repeatedly the estimates made by the economic planners have proved to be too conservative, and economic plans have had to be revised long before the expiration of the planning period.

Both the dynamic nature of the private sector and uncertainty about growth have put real limitations on the use of economic plans for determining the level of investment in individual sectors of the economy. And in fact government plans have been revised frequently.

Economic planners in Japan have emphasized the importance of planning as a guide for making current decisions with long-term ramifications. Such an understanding is especially important for Japan because it was undergoing a far-reaching and rapid structural transformation. Japan was changing from a labor-surplus to a labor-shortage economy, from an economy with a low income to one with a high income, and from one with large premodern elements to one with a modernized economic structure.

It is useful to predict in a government plan the direction of major changes in agriculture, industry, foreign trade, and people's daily lives; to indicate possible bottlenecks and imbalances that may arise; and to determine the long-term policies necessary to meet these changes.

The plan also helps individuals and enterprises to evaluate how changes in the national economy will affect them in the long run. Thus the plan introduces macroeconomic concepts into personal thinking and has worked to reduce sharp political differences among the various groups in the Japanese economy.

In general, economic planning has not been designed to stimulate rapid growth but rather to attain balanced growth and indicate the long-term economic policy.

Economic Plans and Their Impact
Since the end of World War II several economic plans with a variety of objectives have been prepared in Japan. Indeed, all of these plans were formulated with a view toward

securing a continuous increase in per-capita income and achieving a full-employment economy, but they put emphasis on different objectives in accordance with the stages of recovery and development of the economy.

The plans prepared by the Japanese government so far can be classified into three groups: plans in the rehabilitation stage, plans for the self-supporting economy, and plans in the development stage.

The first group of economic plans focused on the reconstruction of the war-damaged economy. World War II seriously isolated Japan from external economic markets, cutting its imports from the traditional sources of supplies, destroying the greater part of its transportation and communications facilities, and creating a high level of unemployment. Economic activities fell sharply below the level prevailing during the 1930s.

In 1946 the Economic Stabilization Board, which was later reorganized as the Economic Deliberation Board (1952) and subsequently changed to the present Economic Planning Agency (1954), was established on the recommendation of the Allied Occupation Forces to stabilize and reconstruct the economy. To this board a special council charged with the task of preparing a reconstruction plan was attached. This council prepared a report, "Economic Rehabilitation Plan, 1949–1953," in 1948. This draft was never officially adopted by the government because of political changes in the cabinet, but it provided background information for the government in requesting economic aid from the United States. This period of recovery lasted nearly five years until the onset of the Korean War in 1950.

Japan received nearly $2 billion in economic aid in the five years following defeat. It also had a windfall from the U.S. Army's special procurements of commodities and services during the Korean War—a source of foreign exchange that bridged the gap between normal exports and import requirements. In 1953, for example, this source of dollar revenue amounted to $800 million and financed nearly half of the $1.6 billion in imports.

The Three-Year Economic Plan of 1952 and the Five-Year Plan for Economic Self-Support of 1955 were prepared with the goal of attaining a self-supporting economy. The latter's target was to attain a 5 percent growth rate in the GNP during the period 1956–1960. Industrial policies centered on the modernization of export industries and the promotion of industries that would reduce import dependency. Machinery, chemical products, and synthetic textiles were designated promising industries with long-term loans being offered at a preferentially low rate of interest. Shortly after the preparation of the plan, however, the economy experienced a boom, with a growth rate nearly double the plan target, and many of the five-year targets were attained in only two years.

In 1957 industry recovered to its prewar (1934–1936 average) level, and the economy passed from the recovery stage into a new development stage. In December 1957 the New Long-Range Economic Plan was prepared with the objective of "providing for a steady increase in the standard of living and providing for full employment with the maximum rate of economic growth consistent with economic stability." The plan stated:

Based on the character of the plan, it is necessary to restrict to the minimum government direct control measures and give free rein to private enterprises as much as possible—recognizing that it is the motive power for the development of the economy. The government also must establish long-range measures for undertaking projects which are difficult for private enterprise to carry out. That is, the government must reinforce social overhead capital such as roads, railways, and port facilities.

The plan set an annual growth rate of 6.5 percent as the most feasible and for the first time estimated detailed gross investment in basic public facilities.

The actual course of growth was again underestimated. The annual rate of growth of GNP from 1958 through 1960 was about 10 percent, far exceeding the plan target of 6.5 percent.There are several reasons for this:

1. The terms of trade turned in Japan's favor by over 10 percent due to an unexpected 15 percent drop in the import price index over three years. This fact permitted larger imports with a given amount of exports.

2. The rate of growth of gross capital formation rose to over 35 percent of GNP in both 1959 and 1960, compared with the planned rate of 28.5 percent for 1962. A larger supply of capital made possible a higher rate of growth.

3. Industrial production, particularly in the machinery industry, expanded much faster than expected.

The National Income Doubling Plan and Its Impact

In November 1959 Prime Minister Nobusuke Kishi requested the Economic Deliberation Council (the Secretariat of which was the Economic Planning Agency) to draft a new plan for doubling national income. The council worked out a draft and presented it to the government (Ikeda cabinet) in late 1960 after extensive study. Based on this draft, the government officially adopted the Plan for Doubling National Income in December 1960.

This plan aimed to double the national income within the next decade and set a 7 to 8 percent annual growth rate as both feasible and realistic. The plan emphasized five points:

1. Strengthening of social overhead capital. With a rapid expansion of the private sector, public facilities such as roads, harbors, and water supply had become serious hindrances to further economic growth. It was necessary to

restore a balance between the private and public sectors by accelerating social overhead investment. The ratio of investment in basic public facilities to enterprise investment was to be raised from one to three to one to two by 1970.

2. Inducements to industrialization. The plan considered secondary industry the leading sector for growth. It emphasized the growth of the heavy metals, chemical and machinery industries as strategic sectors. Although the attainment of these objectives mainly rested with private business, government provided inducements with special tax provisions and the active use of government financial institutions.

3. Promotion of exports. The plan assumed a 10 percent average annual increase in exports. A high rate of growth for exports was needed to compensate for an expected decline in special procurement dollar receipts from the United States and a rise in imports due to liberalization of imports. The plan assumed that the share of machinery products (including vehicles) in total exports would rise from 24 percent in 1959 to 37 percent in 1970.

4. Development of human ability and the advancement of science and technology. The plan emphasized the importance of human factors in economic growth. It assumed an increase in public and private research expenditures from 0.9 to 2.0 percent of GNP. The plan also set targets for the number of university graduates in science and technology, college graduates in engineering, and vocational trainees.

5. Mitigation of the dual structure and securing of social ability. One of Japan's peculiar characteristics is the coexistence of modern and premodern sectors. There have been wide differentials in wages and income among various sectors of the economy. This structure has, in part, supported the competitive strength of Japan's exports and a high rate of savings, but it is also a source of inequality and backwardness. Moreover, as the economy modernized, it had become a hindrance to higher efficiency and techno-

logical progress. Therefore the plan emphasized the importance of mitigating this dual structure.

The plan had several other features. It covered the ten years from 1961 to 1970 and described the long-range prospects of the national economy to facilitate the preparation of individual plans by various government agencies. In this connection a long-range investment program in the public sector was seen as a useful means for attaining the objectives of the plan.

In 1954, when the government had no long-range economic plan and faced a balance-of-payments crisis, it curtailed public investment without giving due consideration to the long-term implications. The introduction of planning, especially in the public sector, prevented sharp fluctuations in government expenditures when the economy later experienced similar balance-of-payments problems.

The plan divided the economy into two sectors: the public sector, for which the government is directly responsible, and the private sector, in which private enterprises have responsibilities and initiatives. The plan for the public sector included an allocation of funds for major public works that linked the long-term economic plan with fiscal budgeting.

Since Japanese planning aims principally at providing guidelines for economic activities to be conducted by free enterprise, the plan did not give detailed targets for every sector of the economy but instead emphasized long-term policy measures.

For the first time in postwar planning, problems related to income differentials among different groups of people, differentials between large and small enterprises in productivity and wages, and regional differences in incomes became important. Following this overall national plan, the government worked out a new regional development plan in October 1962, with one of its major purposes being to overcome the excessive differentials in income among various regions of the country.

The importance of the human factor in economic development was also emphasized. A Committee for Education and Training was set up as one of the seventeen subcommittees working on the preparation of the National Income Doubling Plan. In April 1961 the Committee for Development of Human Resources was set up in accordance with the recommendation, included in the National Income Doubling Plan, to undertake further studies in this field. In January 1963 the committee submitted its report to the government and recommended a labor and education policy for economic development.

Economic planning in Japan has been and still is in the evolutionary stage. Planners are groping for an appropriate type of planning to meet the requirements both of free enterprise and of the basic characteristics of Japan's economy.

Among the general public the work of economic planning has aroused interest in and hope for the future economy and has helped to introduce long-range considerations into the decision-making process of government, private enterprise, and individuals.

There are some shortcomings in Japan's economic planning. The most important one is insufficient quantitative link between the targets of the plan and the policy measures to implement it. Despite these shortcomings, economic planning has become an indispensable element of economic life.

Recent Tendencies of Japan's Economic Plans

The Japanese economy has shown a number of changes since 1970. Three may be singled out as being particularly important to economic planning.

The first is a slowing of economic growth. Japan maintained a high growth rate, nearly 10 percent in real terms,

Table 10.1
Japan's economic growth rates since 1970

Fiscal year (April–March)	Real	Nominal
1970	8.3	15.8
1971	5.3	10.2
1972	9.7	16.6
1973	5.3	21.0
1974	−0.2	18.4
1975	3.6	10.0
1976	5.1	12.2
1977	5.3	10.9
1978	5.1	9.5
1979	5.3	7.4
1980	4.6	8.5
1981	3.5	5.7
1982	3.3	5.0

Source: Economic Planning Agency.

in and after the late 1950s, but growth slowed in the wake of the first oil crisis in 1973, averaging around 5 percent in the 1970s (table 10.1).

There are many reasons for slower economic growth, which include limitations on energy supplies, insufficient work force, intensified environmental problems, greater limitations on plant location, and changes in growth psychology of the society.

The second factor is a change in the relationship between Japan and the world economy. Japan's international position has risen rapidly. Japan accounted for only 2 percent of the world's GNP in 1955 but nearly 10 percent in 1980 (table 10.2). With a growing international interdependence, developments linked to overseas trends in oil, fluctuations in exchange rates, and trade frictions came to affect economic performance seriously.

The third factor is a change in policy priority as the level of national income has risen. Economic independence and higher standard of living were postwar Japan's primary targets. Seeking examples in America and Europe, Japan aimed to introduce technical innovations in the quest of

Table 10.2
Major economies' shares of world GNP (percent)

	1955	1960	1970	1978	1980
Japan	2.2	2.9	6.0	10.0	9.0
United States	36.3	33.7	30.2	21.8	21.5
European Community	17.5	17.5	19.3	20.2	22.4
Soviet Union	13.9	15.2	15.9	13.0	11.6
China	4.4	4.7	4.9	4.6	4.7
World total	100.0	100.0	100.0	100.0	100.0
(billion $)	(1,100)	(1,500)	(3,250)	(9,660)	(12,215)

Source: U.S. President's "International Economic Report" (1977) for 1955–1970 figures and U.S. President's "Economic Report" (1980, 1982) for 1978 and 1980.

economic progress. As a result of its unusually fast growth Japan's economic power and living standards have improved rapidly, reaching levels close to those of the United States and European countries. Given that background, noneconomic aspects such as maintaining a favorable living environment and improving public welfare have come to assume greater importance.

Outlines of Recent Economic Plans
Japan has devised several economic plans in recent years. A plan was drawn up in February 1973, but the growth target and other economic goals in the plan diverged far from reality in the wake of the shift to the floating exchange rate system, the oil crisis, and galloping inflation. A new plan for the second half of the 1970s was drafted in May 1976. A major feature of the plan was a far lower medium-term economic growth target. The plan, prepared amid the worst recession since World War II, focused on a program of recovery. It envisaged that surplus supplies, both industrial and human, would be absorbed by achieving relatively high economic growth in the first half of the five-year plan, and then in the second half the economy would settle down to a moderate but stable growth pattern.

The plan called for an average annual growth rate of about 6 percent. Among its specific targets were price stability and full employment, switching from a conventional growth pattern focused on quantitative expansion to a quality-first pattern focusing on national life—improving social security, housing, and social overhead capital while stepping up environmental protection.

Again economic performance was considerably different from that envisaged in the plan. The economy did not recover as much as expected despite pump-priming fiscal measures. The economy grew at an annual rate of around 5 percent. Japan's current-account surplus also expanded in 1977–1978, causing strained relations with Japan's trading partners and a steep appreciation of the yen.

As a result work started in 1978 on a new economic plan. In August 1979 a new seven-year socioeconomic plan was drawn up. The plan set forth three basic directions and five goals. The basic directions were correcting imbalances among various sectors of the economy, altering the industrial structure and overcoming limitations on energy supplies, and improving the quality of national life. The five goals were achieving full employment and price stability, stabilizing and improving national life, cooperating in and contributing to the development of the international economic society, ensuring economic security, and laying the groundwork for the development and reconstructing of deficit-ridden state finances.

The plan sought economic growth led by domestic demand centering on public works spending and hoped to restore equilibrium in the international balance of payments. The plan called for administrative and fiscal reforms designed to slash expenses and the introduction of a general excise tax—similar to Europe's value-added tax—aimed at boosting revenues.

Again the economic situation changed after the new seven-year socioeconomic plan was prepared. First, the second oil crisis of 1979 seriously affected the economy.

Because of the deflationary impact of the second oil crisis, economic activity began to stagnate in 1980, resulting in a considerably slower growth rate than the 5.1 percent projected under the plan. Second, the government failed to win public support for its financial reconstruction plan featuring the introduction of a general excise tax. It switched to a policy of balancing the budget mainly through spending cuts. Third, technical innovations centering on electronics have progressed remarkably in recent years. Such progress will have a great effect on employment, the industrial structure, and many other aspects of the economy.

A change in the work force is also apparent. The nation's working population has been increasing more rapidly than envisaged because of a remarkable rise in the number of working women. The unemployment rate has been running above the plan's 1.7 percent projection, due to such changes as well as to slower economic expansion.

To cope with these changes, the government decided to map out a new five-year plan, with fiscal 1983 as a starting year. The Economic Council, a panel of economic advisers to the government, began work on the new plan in July 1982, and the "Economic and Social Outlook and Policy Guidelines" was announced by the government in August 1983. Key points of the new plan were devoted to maintaining flexibility of the economy, reducing the huge budget deficit, and showing future directions for structural change.

Before preparing the latest plan mentioned, the Economic Council set up a Long-Term Outlook Committee. The committee looked at Japan's economy and society from a long-term perspective and considered the options necessary to cope with problems that will arise in the course of change.

In June 1982 the committee which I chaired presented its report entitled, "Japan in the Year 2000—Preparing Japan for an Age of Internationalization, the Aging Society, and Maturity." The report regards the rest of the twentieth century as a historic turning point for Japan's economy and society. It points out that Japan must resolve many problems in the broad trend toward internationalization of the economy and society, aging of the population, and maturing of the industrial structure.

Changing Undercurrent of Economic Plans
Japan is a country with a free economy where resources are distributed by private companies and consumers conduct transactions through the marketplace. Competition is intense, and the market mechanism is strong. What role does economic planning play against such a background? In 1969 the Economic Council set up a committee to study the roles to be played by economic planning. The committee singled out three points. The first role is to enlighten the public by focusing attention on economic projection. An economic plan shows a blueprint of a future economy; businesses can map out their own long-term plans using the economic plan as a yardstick. The second role is to carry out, as a long-term government promise, specific policy programs such as investment in social overhead capital. The third role is to function as a forum for adjusting conflicting interests. The economic council that discusses economic plans consists of businessmen, labor representatives, journalists, and economists. These parties have conflicting interests, but in the course of discussions they narrow the differences of their views on what Japan's economy and society should look like in the long run.

Where are Long-Term Economic Policies Headed?

Industrial Policy   Japan has an industrial structure policy, in which MITI (the Ministry of International Trade and Industry) has played an important role. The government continuously discusses what industries should lead Japan's economic activity at every stage of economic development. Emphasis was placed on the reconstruction of industries producing basic materials such as steel and coal in the 1950s and on heavy and chemical industries during the high-growth period in the 1960s. The "Japan in the Year 2000" report points to "softwarization" (a combination of knowledge-intensive and service industries) as a direction in which Japan's industrial structure move. Such a policy of providing "vision" of the future, while leaving structural change basically to the forces of the market, seeks to smooth the process of adjustment. It is designed to help develop industries with growth potential and organize an orderly retreat of industries on the wane.

In the future Japan will continue to encounter industrial adjustments in labor-intensive and basic-material industries due to growing competition from newly industrialized countries. Industrial adjustments in the high-growth period were relatively easy to make because the economy was expanding rapidly, permitting workers of decaying industries to be easily absorbed in growth industries. With slower economic growth industrial adjustments may be harder in the future.

Technological Development   Japan adopted a policy of encouraging technology imports in the 1950s, but as it caught up with Western industrial countries, priority has shifted to self-developed technology. In general the government does not play a major role in technological development. As shown in table 10.3, the Japanese government shoulders a low rate of expenses to total research and development costs, even excluding spending on defense R & D.

Japan's technological development has been pushed chiefly by the private sector. It is often pointed out that Japan is weak in the development of fundamental technology and strong in application or that it is good at improving an acquired technique little by little rather than creating original technology. But the conventional practice of growing in applied areas, while depending on technologies in-

Table 10.3
Government share of research and development costs

	Total R & D spending (billion yen)	Defense R & D costs (billion yen)	Government share (percent)	Excepting defense (percent)
Japan (1979)	4,063.6	27.6	27.4	26.9
United States (1979)	11,896.2	2,661.0	49.3	34.7
West Germany (1978)	3,185.1	181.5	46.7	43.5
France (1979)	2,240.7	481.6	58.4	47.0
Britain (1978)	1,313.0	371.7	49.2	29.2

Source: Science and Technology Agency: *Handbook of Science and Technology Statistics.*

troduced from abroad, will reach its limit in the future. Japan will need to develop original technology on its own.

Financial Policy   Japan's financial policy also faces a major turning point. The wave of *internationalization* is spreading to the financial front. Japan has a high savings rate, but it is expected to decline gradually in the future along with the aging of the population. Japan, however, is expected to maintain for some years to come its relatively high savings rate compared with other industrial nations. As the ratio of economic growth has come down from 10 percent in the 1960s to 4 percent in the 1980s, there is the structural surplus of domestic savings which is reflected in the large surplus of Japan's balance of payments. This will mean that Japan will become one of the important sources of supplying capital to the world.

Japan is expected to shift to the exportation of capital, and in the course of this shift capital transactions will be liberalized, causing the domestic financial system to change as well.

Japan in the Year 2000

Since the Meiji restoration in 1868, Japan has used the advanced countries of the West as its model for modernization. The goal shared by all Japanese was to catch up with these countries, and the Japanese people made tremendous efforts to achieve this goal. Japan now accounts for one-tenth of the world economic output.

But the next twenty years will constitute a period of historic transition. In demographic terms this will be a period of aging as the postwar baby boom generation reaches middle and advanced age. But since the ratio of the productive-age population will not change substantially in the next twenty years, Japan has time to prepare for a society with a large proportion of elderly citizens.

In terms of growth this will be a period of medium growth, slightly higher than that of the advanced countries of the West. Japan's international position will continue to rise gradually, and the country will play an increasingly important role in meeting the world's economic problems. At the same time Japan will be required to build a more open economic society.

The phase of catching up with the advanced countries of the West has ended, and the country has entered a stage of maturity. It can be said that this is the stage similar to a man's maturity or prime of life, the period of perfecting the inner self following the youthful period of absorption and growth. In a period of transition the thinking and attitudes that worked in the past—the concept of catching up with the West, approaching problems with an emphasis on growth, and the "small-nation rationale" of not thinking about the impact of one's behavior on other nations—will no longer be viable.

Since the economic prosperity achieved after World War II will have historical significance only if we are able in the next twenty years to leave posterity a system in tune with the new age—a good social infrastructure and sound international relations—we need a new grand design geared to the next century.

View of the Next Century

For the world economy the 1980s can be viewed as a period of adjustment following a period of confusion in the 1970s. If the world economy adjusts successfully, the 1990s will be a period of multipolar stabilization.

There are many different views on the future of the world economy, but we have made the following basic assumptions in working out our long-term prospects:

1. Although interdependent relations will develop gradually, they will not provide the same stable framework for the world economy as they did in the 1960s.

2. Industrialized nations will not be able to achieve growth rates as high as those in the 1960s even if they should succeed in revitalizing their economy.

3. Although it is unlikely that energy prices will jump so suddenly as to disturb the world economy, the real price of oil will continue to rise gradually.

Under these assumptions, the outlook for the world and Japan's position in the world is expected to be as follows:

1. In the year 2000 Japan's GNP will be 12 percent of the world's total GNP, as compared to 10 percent in 1980.

2. The gap in per capita income between industrialized nations and developing nations will remain wide.

3. Heading toward the twenty-first century, the Asian region has potential for faster growth.

Outlook for Japan

Population
Japan's population will peak at about 130 million in the year 2000 and then decline gradually until it stabilizes. During this period the population pyramid will change shape from the present bell type to the bowl type to the barrel type. At present, one out of eleven persons is aged sixty five or over. In 2000, one out of 6.4 persons will belong to this age bracket. Thus the ratio of productive-age population to the entire population will decline rapidly after 2000. At present, one person of nonproductive age is supported by 1.5 persons of productive age. In 2015, one nonproductive person will have to be supported by 1.2 productive persons. The number of aged persons (women in particular) who have been divorced or widowed will increase.

The rate of increase in the number of ordinary households will slow, while the number of single-member households, in particular those in which an aged woman lives alone, will increase considerably. The ratio of the number of nuclear families to the total number of families will remain as high as it is today. Although people will continue to prefer permanent residence in a particular community, there may be active population movements as a result of the second baby-boom generation's coming of age, the greater dissemination of higher education, and growth of the service economy.

Economic Growth

If Japan can maintain its economic vitality, it should be able to sustain a moderate economic growth slightly higher than the growth of other industrialized nations. The productive-age population in Japan will be high by international comparison and the decline in the savings rate small.

A calculation based on a long-term multisector model shows that Japan's economic growth will be around 4.4 percent if full operation of capital equipment is assumed and around 4 percent if the operation rate is assumed to be near the average of the past.

Savings and Investment

The household savings rate will decrease slowly (down 2 to 4 percent by 2000) but not sharply. It will remain higher than the savings rates in Western nations.

Private equipment investment will be on a level compatible with the moderate growth of the national economy. The capital-output ratio will remain about the same or decrease slightly. Housing investment will increase in the form of improvements in the quality of housing and accumulation of social-overhead capital will continue.

Development of Technology
Vigorous efforts will be continued to develop technology, especially in the field of mechatronics. Increasing emphasis will be given to creative development of technology.

Energy
Japan's total energy demand, which stood at 429 million kiloliters (in terms of oil) in 1980, will increase to 690 million kiloliters by 2000. Because a major increase in oil supply is unlikely, Japan will have to depend in large measure on nuclear energy, in addition to coal, liquid natural gas, and new energy sources.

Industrial Structure
Japan's industrial society will shift its emphasis from materials and resources to knowledge and services. The production shares of the primary and the secondary industries will decrease in nominal terms. The share of service industries will show a remarkable increase in nominal terms. Among the secondary industries the machinery industry including electronics will increase its share greatly.

In agriculture it will become possible in twenty years to lower the prices of farm produce to the level of the European Community through the extensive adoption of new management systems if appropriate measures are taken to expand the scale of agriculture during the process of retirement or death of older (farming) populations. The materials-processing industry, after passing through an adjustment phase in the 1980s, may assume a new aspect in the 1990s by giving emphasis on quality rather than quantity. The processing and assembling industry including electronics has good prospects for growth.

Employment Structure
The labor force will increase by 10 percent in the 1980s and by 3.6 percent in the 1990s, reaching 65 million in 2000, as compared with 57 million in 1980. The number of workers

will decrease sharply in the primary industries, increase slightly in the secondary industries and increase greatly in the tertiary industries. By 2000 one of every two persons will be employed in service industries.

Trade, Overseas Investment

There will be a change in trade structure from vertical specialization to horizontal specialization among East and Southeast Asian countries. With the development of the service economy, trade in services such as finance, insurance, information, and travel will assume greater importance. Overseas direct investment will continue to increase.

Lifestyles

With living standards and the level of education rising, the Japanese will seek spiritual and cultural values in a variety of forms and will have increasing desires for self-fulfillment. They will continue to prefer harmony to confrontation and will try to retain good human relations within a group rather than argue by force of logic. This sentiment may undergo some change in the course of internationalization but will remain in the basic principle of Japanese behavior.

Several changes will take place:

1. Families and communities will play an increasing role in the people's lives.

2. The life cycle will change as life expectancy extends to age eighty. An important problem will be how to spend one's later years after the children become independent.

3. With the reduction of working hours (a five-day work week and a long vacation will become common by 2000), people will have more time to themselves. The total leisure time of the Japanese (aged ten and older) will increase by an annual average of 1.3 percent.

There will be changes in consumer life. Of the total consumer expenditure the proportion of necessary expenditure will decrease, while that of discretionary expenditure will increase. People will engage actively in leisure-time activities. With the electronics-bred generation expanding, technological innovation, particularly in the field of mechatronics, will influence family life in various ways. In-home services will be expanded. Lifelong education and learning will become more widespread.

The population will increase around big cities and in provincial cities. People will seek a living environment that is both diverse and of high quality with emphasis on nature, culture, and fine surroundings. Grandparents, parents, and children may live together as a three-generation family, live separately in the same neighborhood, or choose from among one of many other ways of living.

Three Major Currents

The major changes in the Japanese economy as it moves toward the next century can be featured by the three major currents of internationalization, aging of the population, and maturity.

Internationalization

So far internationalization has progressed in the areas where it is easily acceptable, mainly in the economy. In the future, however, internationalization will progress in diverse fields in a manner that will affect the very pattern of Japanese life.

As internationalization progresses, several developments will take place. International division of labor will progress through foreign trade, and new trade frictions will arise among the advanced countries. Japanese industry also has to adjust its structure to respond to the progress of industrialization in developing countries. The flow of capital will become more lively, and the internationalization of the yen will progress.

Internationalization cannot be stopped. Japan can ensure its own development only by maintaining friendly relations with the rest of the world. It must cope positively with internationalization.

First, Japan must contribute to the revitalization of the world economy and the creation of a positive-sum situation. In order to achieve this, it is necessary to establish an international economic system with new rules befitting a new age on the basis of free trade, to channel the dynamism of the Japanese economy into revitalizing the world economy by achieving economic growth led by domestic demand, and to strengthen the economic solidarity of the Pacific basin nations.

Second, Japan must make its economic society more open internationally. Japan will need to carry out its industrial adjustment smoothly while opening up its market further to remodel its domestic system into one better suited to internationalization.

Third, Japan should vigorously address global problems of importance such as the North–South problem, the food problem, and the environmental problem. Japan must strive for disarmament by maintaining and promoting a peaceful international environment.

Aging of Population

The first problem that arises from the aging of the population is how to provide adequate job opportunities to the rapidly growing labor force of the aged, particularly people of fifty-five and over. If the past trends of employment by age group should continue, it is likely that the supply of elderly workers will exceed demand.

Then there is the problem of social security. If the present programs remain as they are, the ratio of social security contributions to national income will rise sharply, adversely affecting the incentive to work of the working age population.

Thus it is very important to provide opportunities for the aged to participate in economic and social activities by making the best use of their experiences, and to provide adequate public welfare services by revising the pension system.

In this connection we should not overlook the fact that the aged people in Japan have a stronger desire to work compared with the elderly in other industrialized countries.

Maturity

An important problem that requires the utmost attention in the process of maturity is how to prevent a loss of the vitality of Japan's economy and society, under the condition of rather moderate economic growth and aging of the population.

In order to maintain the vitality, it is necessary to promote the development of original technology, since import of technology will gradually become difficult.

It is also necessary to improve the social framework so that the vitality of the private sector could be allowed full play, through maintaining competitive environment by curbing possible tendency toward oligopolistic control of the market, through correct evaluation, and modification, if necessary, of Japan's business and employment practices, and through encouragement of new responses by medium and small enterprises.

Conclusion

The next twenty years will be exceptionally important to Japan's economy. With internationalization, an aging population, and maturity, the road facing Japan's economy is not necessarily smooth, but it is certainly possible to solve the problems that will occur in the future. It is important to bequeath to future generations not just a vigorous economy but a population motivated to work, a sense of consid-

eration for others, and a spirit of overcoming difficulties by
putting their intelligence to work. It is the responsibility
and duty of those of us who live in the present to build such
a society and to pass it on to the next generation.

Lester Thurow
Reblending the American Economic Mixture

Consider the five elements in the Japanese economic strategy at the beginning of the income-doubling decade:
strengthen social overhead capital, push growth industries,
promote exports, develop human ability and technology,
and secure social stability by mitigating the dual structure
of the economy. This list could easily serve as strategic
objectives for the American economy by the year 2000.

A vigorous economy requires a good infrastructure for
transportation of goods and services. No one believes that
America now has that infrastructure in place. In an
economy that has ground to a halt and has a more than
fifteen-year history of falling rates of growth of productivity, clearly we have to do something to push our growth
industries. Growth is not happening automatically.

In a country now dependent on imports to maintain its
standard of living, exports have to grow. There are two
ways for this to occur: we can learn to compete against the
world's best in promoting exports, or we can let the value of
our currency fall and watch our standard of living fall behind that of the rest of the world.

America is now being outproduced in terms of engineers
and other scientific personnel, and we now spend less on
civilian research and development than do our major international competitors. Does anyone really believe that we
can compete as equals as long as this is occurring?

Given an average black family income only slightly more
than half that of the average white family income, can anyone deny the importance of eliminating the dual structure

between rich and poor in our economy? It might be noted that the degree of inequality in the Japanese distribution of family income is less than half that in the American distribution of family income. Equality versus efficiency is not a necessary dichotomy either.

Perhaps we need to take seriously what Saburo Okita writes elsewhere about Japan in the year 2000: "Whether the economic prosperity achieved since World War II will have historical significance will depend on whether we shall be able in the next twenty years to leave to posterity a system in tune with the new age, a good *social* infrastructure stock, and sound international relations." *We need a new grand design geared to the next century.*

What is the new grand design for the American twenty-first century? Do we have to have one? What happens if we do not? In the past it was taken as axiomatic that America had a manifest destiny with economic success. But does it? No one knows, but given our economic troubles over the past two decades, there is room to wonder.

11

The Japanese Economy: Present and Future

Hisao Kanamori

In 1955 Japan's economy was 2.2 percent of the world economy and one-seventeenth that of the United States. By 1980 it had expanded to 10 percent of the world economy and half that of the United States. Japan's growth rate dropped by half to 5 percent in the 1970s, but even then it was higher than that of other developed countries. Why was it so high? Will it continue to be so?

Rapid Growth in 1960s

Japan's high growth rate can be explained from a variety of perspectives—political, cultural, social, or economic. I shall try to explain Japan's growth mainly from an economic viewpoint but providing some social observation. According to the neoclassical growth theory, growth rates are the summation of increases in labor inputs, increases in capital inputs, and increases in productivity.

Increase in Labor Force

During the 1960s Japan increased its labor input at an annual rate of 2.2 percent. This growth can be explained by the following:

1. *The absorption of excess labor after the war*   The postwar economic recovery was not enough to create full employment, but unemployed labor was gradually absorbed as recovery quickened.

2. *A rise in the birth rate*   Japan had a postwar baby boom from 1947 to 1949; the birth rate was 3.4 percent, about double Japan's average. These children entered the labor force in the 1960s.

3. *The rise of educational standards*   After the war more young people went on to higher education, upgrading the quality of the labor force. The ratio of high school and university graduates among the male labor force rose from 7 percent in 1960 to 14 percent in 1970.

4. *Compositional changes in the labor force*   Male workers in the age group between 20 and 64 increased.

Increase in Capital

Capital increased in the 1960s at the annual rate of 11 percent—very much higher than that of other countries. The rate of savings was an important element in this.

In the 1960s Japan's savings rate was extremely high (about 40 percent of GNP). Savings can be divided into three categories: household savings, enterprise savings, and savings by the government. In each category Japan's savings rates were very high.

The average household saved almost 20 percent of its total aftertax income—much higher than the 5 percent in the United States or Great Britain. There are a number of reasons for this: (1) a general habit of the Japanese people, (2) high growth rate but consumption lagging behind the rise in income, (3) inadequate social security system causing people to prepare themselves financially for disease and old age, (4) low ownership of houses and financial assets with people saving as much as they can to buy a home.

Enterprises retained a large portion of their profits because we have few individual stockholders and because banks and insurance companies have greater influence among the stockholders. These so-called institutional investors wanted to reserve their profits and to use them to provide for enterprise growth rather than to distribute them among stockholders as dividends.

Government savings was high because there was little expenditure for public consumption such as for social security and armaments. Taxes were 20 percent of the national income in Japan, the lowest among developed countries, and government could save a considerable portion of its annual income.

The rate of investment in housing was also low, leaving most funds available for productive purposes. These investments enabled new technologies to be employed.

Rise of Productivity

Productivity was the biggest contributor to growth in the 1960s—6.6 percent of the 10.6 percent growth rate was due to the rise of productivity. Here I do not mean labor or capital productivity but the total factor productivity of both labor and capital. In short, Japan's economy grew not only because the volume of the labor and the capital rose but also because of the rapid rise in its productivity.

This rise is explained partially by the fact that labor and capital moved from agriculture and self-supporting enterprises with low productivity to manufacturing and big businesses with higher productivity. But the most important reason was innovation.

Some postwar structural changes enabled these changes to take place—land reform abolished landlordship and created landed farmers, the *zaibatsus* were dissolved, and labor unions were organized.

After Japan regained its independence in the late 1950s new technologies were introduced from the United States. Gradually new products—synthetic fibers, petrochemical products, transistor radios, television sets, and computers—appeared. New productive methods were introduced—integrated steel production systems, new refineries, the petrochemical *kombinat* system, and mass production of automobiles. New markets for durable goods were developed, first in cities and then in rural areas.

Since with land reform the income of farmers had risen, rural areas became large consumers, in particular of automobiles which are more abundant there than in urban areas. Once the local market was developed and mass production was in full swing, industry proceeded to produce for the American market, with more than half of all television sets and automobiles earmarked for export. And in the field of energy there was a dramatic conversion from coal to oil, which at first lowered the cost of energy.

Innovation proceeded rapidly in Japan for three reasons: effective leadership, technological progress, and the wide social acceptance of innovation. After the war new entrepreneurs appeared in Japan spurred on by the dissolution of *zaibatsus,* enactment of the antimonopoly law, and ever more opportunities for competition. Innovation always brings new leadership, and that happened in postwar Japan. Owner-managers, managers of large enterprises, and technocrats like middle managers and engineers all promoted innovation. Even bureaucrats played a role. Farmers, who were usually regarded as conservative, were progressive in improving seeds, introducing machines, and organizing sales networks. Farmers, who had become landowners because of the land reform, were now entrepreneurs. Indeed, the rise of productivity after the war was higher in agriculture than in manufacturing.

Social acceptance was important. In Japan consumers showed a positive interest in new products. Labor unions were also favorable to innovation. In Western countries the biggest bottleneck for innovation is labor unions who spurn technological change. In the West, for example, it is difficult to introduce computers into production because workers fear that the use of these machines will lead to unemployment. But in Japan, labor unions are quite positive to the introduction of robots. Japanese unions tend to leave dangerous or unpleasant jobs to robots or other machines. In addition Japanese workers may have a greater ability to master new machines because of their comparatively higher standard of education.

Strong Growth of Demand

High growth was supported by the increase in consumer demand—a demand that built up during the war and then finally exploded. Equipment investment after 1955 led to a technological transformation as enterprises vigorously competed against each other, encouraged by the dissolution of *zaibatsus* and the end of monopoly.

Banks were eager to lend, and government encouraged investment by easing the corporate taxes. As profits increased with high growth, enterprises became optimistic, and that in turn promoted even more investment.

Exports were another important driving force. As domestic markets rapidly expanded, mass-production systems were employed, and they lowered costs. The manufacturing structure began to shift from textiles and general merchandise to durable goods—steel, automobiles, and machinery. This trend matched the direction of overseas demand and encouraged exports. By the 1960s makers of steel, household durables, and automobiles were strong enough to find and develop markets in America.

The yen foreign exchange was fixed at 360 yen to the dollar in 1949, and it remained unchanged until 1971. As a result Japanese industrial products gained competitiveness in export markets as productivity rose. It is doubtful whether the yen's exchange rate helped to develop Japan's standard of living (it forced Japan to buy raw materials and food at high prices), but it certainly helped Japan expand its exports.

Housing
One area lagged considerably behind—investment in housing especially in urban areas because of the rise in the price of land. This problem has not yet been solved.

Regulation of Supply and Demand by Government
An economy that grows rapidly tends to develop bottlenecks. Japan had recessions in 1954, 1958, 1962, 1965, and 1971 because investment rose too rapidly. At these times government increased demand by easing taxes, lowering bank rates, and increasing public investments. When there was excess demand, policymakers raised taxes, tightened financial markets, and restrained public investments.

These Keynesian policies seemed to have been successful for three reasons. Government action was quick with no time lag between decision and execution. Because enterprises borrow from banks and banks borrow from the Bank of Japan, as the Bank of Japan tightened credit, it immediately affected all enterprises. Agreements between enterprises and unions on wages did little to offset the effect of government policies.

Roles of Market and Government
It is often said that government played a large role in developing Japan's economy. But I believe that the development of Japan's economy was due mainly to innovation in the private sector. Government's role centered on assisting the free activities of private enterprises.

Government adopted an economic planning system immediately after the war. These programs had no direct enforcing power on enterprises and often were altered two or three years after their start. Some criticize the Japanese economic plans as only window dressing with no substantial meaning, but I believe that such plans contributed to the development of Japan's economy. First, they became the foundation of various public policies like road building, port facilities, and social security. Second, private enterprise took these plans into consideration when they planned new investments. Third, they strengthened the consciousness of top enterprises, unions, consumer organizations, and academics who participated in drawing up the long-range plans.

Another unique relationship between the government and enterprises exists in Japan's famous *gyosei-shido*, "administrative guidance." When fears arose that private enterprises were overinvesting, the government often persuaded the enterprises to postpone their investment. Administrative guidance was used in various areas of economy activity in the 1960s. The Bank of Japan also could intercept lending from city banks.

It is difficult to evaluate the effects of these direct interferences by the government and the Bank of Japan. In retrospect, they seem to have been done rather wisely. But the effects of administrative guidance should not be overestimated.

Low Growth in 1970s

Japan's economic growth rate was cut in half in the 1970s (5 percent versus 10 percent in the 1960s), and it had decreased by another 2 to 3 percent in the early 1980s. There is disagreement as to whether this is merely the aftereffect of the oil crisis or the result of a decline in Japan's growth potential.

I believe it is the former. The price of imported crude oil rose fourteen times as fast after the first oil crisis in 1972 as before. The oil increase was a great shock to Japan since it depends on imported oil for more than 70 percent of its energy.

Other worries center around the trade balance. Japan had a large deficit in its trade balance due to the rapid rise in the price of oil in early 1974. Domestic purchasing power was drained by this transfer overseas and individual consumption stagnated. Because of the rise in oil prices, major industries such as aluminum smelting and petrochemicals became noncompetitive.

Nevertheless, Japan's economy seems to have weathered these difficulties. It succeeded in overcoming insufficient oil supplies with conservation. Even steel and other oil-consuming industries cut back remarkably. Alternatives to oil were developed. As a result the GNP rose 35 percent while oil consumption decreased 21 percent. In 1981 the economy needed only about 60 percent of the oil consumed in 1973 per unit of GNP.

The deficit in the trade balance also disappeared as exports increased. And in fact the trade surplus was now so great that it is an international problem.

Inflation was overcome too. The first oil crisis in 1974 triggered a wage explosion because of a rapid rise in wholesale and retail prices, but increases in wages after that were rather gentle and compatible with the rise in labor productivity. Thus a spiraling rise of prices and wages was avoided, and in early 1982 the rate of rise in both wholesale and consumer prices was only 2 percent.

Another aftereffect of the oil crisis is still quite serious, however. The national deficit has become too large. And it is now difficult to increase demand by expanding the public investment.

There are also problems with labor—the wider adoption of the five-day week, a shortening of working hours, an aging labor force, and a growing proportion of female labor. But the quality of labor continues to rise. Among male workers university graduates comprised 23 percent of the labor force in 1980, and this figure is expected to rise to 27 percent in 1990. More female workers have also entered the labor force, and with the rising retirement age, the labor force is expected to increase dramatically. Currently the rate of increase of the labor force continues to be between 1 percent and 2 percent annually, not much different from the 1970s.

Investments in equipment were stagnant in 1981 because of a second oil crisis, but since then there have been new investments to revive technological progress and to rationalize the industrial structure. If investment in equipment increases at an annual rate of 7 percent, the capital stock will increase at a rate of 6.5 percent.

The most important factor is the rate of technological progress. I assume that in the 1980s we shall see a great advance in technology because of electronics. Already we have new products like microcomputers and robots. Revolutionary production methods will appear. It is fortunate that Japan's traditional labor relations—enterprise unionism and lifetime employment—make it easier to adopt new technologies in production.

In the early 1980s there is a desire among Japan's leaders to reform an overgrown administrative system. If this reform succeeds, outmoded organizations will be discarded and new vitality will prevail. But all of these things belong to the future, they are not inevitable. Nevertheless, judging from Japan's history, the possibility for success is not small.

Economic growth cannot be realized without a parallel growth in supply and demand. However high the savings rate and the capital increase, if the demand is not sufficient, there will be no investment in equipment and no innovation. Unions would be concerned about unemployment and oppose the introduction of new technologies. Clearly, many have reason to worry about sufficient demand in the 1980s. Today consumer demands are nearing the saturation point. Investments in equipment are not increasing much. Public investment cannot expand because of the national deficit. Exports are nearing the limits where further exports would certainly invite international friction. In fact Japan's economy may not be able to grow. But I believe this view is too pessimistic.

If the economy stagnates, it will be caused by one of three reasons. The first one is Japan's clinging to an outmoded theory of balanced budgets and ignoring the problem of stimulating demand. Already support for a balanced-budget policy has brought on restraints in public investments and tax increases amid insufficient demand growth. The growth rate of Japan's economy dropped to the 2 percent level in 1981 and 1982 due to deflationary policies designed to ease the national debt. If this policy is continued, investments in equipment will fall and with it growth.

There are also failures in our structural reforms. Japan needs structural reform in its agriculture, cities, and industry. The postwar agricultural land reform contributed to the rise of agricultural productivity, but so many farmers now own small plots of land that productivity is hampered. Too much urbanization has caused the price of land to rise, and urban housing construction is extremely difficult. Oil price hikes have impaired the productivity of aluminum smelters and petrochemicals. If we fail to solve these structural problems, the growth rate will decline.

Japan faces a number of problems in its economic relations with the rest of the world. Can Japan expand its share of a stagnant world export market? Can Japan continue its trade pattern of having an excess of imports over exports from the Middle East and an excess of exports over imports to Europe and America? Is it necessary for Japan to coordinate its economy with the world economy by contributing to world development through investments abroad, by increasing imports of agricultural products, through trade liberalization, and by diversifying its exports? The future of Japan's economy depends on whether we can solve these problems. I cannot predict, but my trust in the adaptability of Japan's economy makes me optimistic.

I concur with the view of the Economic Planning Agency that the average annual growth rate of Japan's economy until 2000 will be around 4 percent.

Lester Thurow
Reblending the American Economic Mixture

A high-quality economy, like a high-quality product, must be built out of high-quality components. There is no way to turn a low-quality product into a high-quality product or a low-quality economy into a high-quality economy. To succeed, each component has to be tuned up and manufactured to tighter tolerances.

The Japanese savings rate is high, but it is high for a number of reasons. Housing and consumer credit were discouraged. For historical reasons government spending on consumption and social welfare programs was low. Defense expenditures did not absorb a large fraction of the GNP. There was no overarching single cause; rather, a number of factors contributed to pushing the Japanese savings rate up to the world's highest.

The Japanese are the world's best at innovation even if many of the basic ideas came from abroad. The trick to social or economic innovation is not a good technical idea but a mechanism whereby it can be brought into actual use in the economy. Consider the computer printing of newspapers. In many European countries unions have prevented the introduction of the new technology, not because they are abstractly against progress but because they concretely fear for their own jobs. In America the new printing technology is widely used but often with union requirements that extra workers be kept on the payroll. America gets more productivity out of computer printing than Europe, but not all of the gains that it could get. The problem is not technical knowledge or innovation but social innovation.

The same problem arises with robots. Japan leads the world in robots, not because it invented the technology, not because it put more money into research and development, and not because its managers are more progressive but because robots are not seen as a threat by the work force, as they are in much of Europe and America.

The Japanese emphasis on consensus building is important for a number of reasons. One of its functions is to make changes less frightening—one gets a chance to talk about it before it happens—and it ensures that those injured or forced to make changes do not suffer all of the economic losses associated with any change. The solution is to make individual goals congruent as much as possible with social goals. Not many of us are willing to lower our standard of living to raise the standard of living of the average American. This is as true in Japan as in the United States. Japanese farmers protest against free trade in agriculture even though it would clearly raise the average real Japanese standard of living and make the international problems of the Japanese economy much easier to solve.

Such conflicts are inevitable, but the goal is to minimize their number and maximize the situations where what is good for the economy is good for the individual. In many ways the Japanese system can be seen as one where the social costs of change are absorbed collectively rather than forcing those costs on individual members of the society. In a pure market economy individuals would have no choice but to accept the costs thrust upon them. But in a political economy there is always recourse to the political process to avoid the costs of change. Such recourse is unavoidable in a democracy. The problem is to channel it in such a direction that progress itself is not halted.

By abolishing the trade assistance adjustment act and the help that it gave to workers unemployed because of international trade at the beginning of the Reagan administration, we increased the pressures for protection. Whatever the problems in running fair trade adjustment payments, they are likely to be small when compared to the costs of an international trade war.

Index